Robert P. M. Ames

Official Report of the Relief Furnished

to the Ohio River flood sufferers, Evansville, Ind., to Cairo, Ills, with the

two trips of the U.S. relief boat Carrie Caldwell, February and March, 1884

Robert P. M. Ames

Official Report of the Relief Furnished
to the Ohio River flood sufferers, Evansville, Ind., to Cairo, Ills, with the two trips of the U.S. relief boat Carrie Caldwell, February and March, 1884

ISBN/EAN: 9783337198442

Printed in Europe, USA, Canada, Australia, Japan

Cover: Foto ©Suzi / pixelio.de

More available books at **www.hansebooks.com**

OFFICIAL REPORT

OF THE

f Furnish

TO THE

FLOOD S

le. Ind., to Ca

WITH THE

WO TRIP

OF THE

S. Relief Boat Carrie

February and March, 1

O MENTION OF OTHER RELIEF, GEN
ON THE FLOOD, CAUSES, AVERTI

BY

R. P. M. AMES, A. M.,

Assistant Surgeon U. S. Marine Hospital S
EVANSVILLE, INDIANA.

ERRATA.

Pa█████ ██████Read for John V. Ha████████████
Hamil█████
█████████████Read for page on, page███████

PREFACE.

The object of this report is to show the entire relief furnished by boats to the sufferers from the great Ohio River flood of 1884, between Evansville, Indiana, and Cairo, Illinois. Had time and space permitted I should have prepared a full and detailed report of all the relief furnished both by the Government and private parties to the sufferers from the headwaters of the Ohio to its mouth. A brief mention will, however, be found of the principal portion of this relief with a few remarks upon the causes of the floods, the probability of averting them, and a detailed log of the two trips of the U. S. Relief Boat Carrie Caldwell from Evansville, Indiana, to Cairo, Illinois. In preparing this report I am indebted to Honorable Robert T. Lincoln, Secretary of War; Honorable Charles J. Folger, Secretary of the Treasury, and Dr. John V. Hamilton, Surgeon General of the U. S. Marine Hospital Service. For my weather report I am indebted to Brigadier and Brevet Major General W. B. Hazen, Chief Signal Officer U. S. A. and to the following officers of the U. S. Signal service:

O. D. STEWART, Pittsburgh, Pa.

L. DUNNE, Cincinnati, Ohio.

E. B. GARRIOTT, Louisville, Ky.

W. H. RAY, CAIRO, Illinois.

Also to A. H. Beach, Surveyor of Customs, Wheeling, West Virginia, Dr. W. H. P. Stoddard, Evansville, Indiana, S A. Whitfield, Postmaster at Cincinnati, V. C. Thompson, Postmaster at Louisville, and Rev. E. R. Donehoo, Pittsburgh, Pa.

To Honorable William Heilman, of Evansville, Ind., I am under many obligations for information contained in this report;
also to James H. McNeeley, of the Evansville Journal, and Mr.
William Caldwell, of Evansville. To Mr. N. S. Byram, Chairman of the Indianapolis Board of Trade Relief Committee I am
obliged for the information relative to the relief rendered by
that Committee; also to Miss Clara Barton, President of the
American Red Cross Association, and for assistance in collect-
ing data on the Lower Ohio I am indebted to Mayor T. C.
Bridwell, of Evansville, Mayor Charles Reed, of Paducah, Ky.,
and to Mayor Wm. P. Halliday, of Cairo, Illinois.

Very Respectfully,

R. P. M. AMES.

CUSTOM HOUSE,
Evansville, Ind.,
May 1, 1884.

GENERAL HISTORY OF THE FLOOD.

THE great flood which swept down the Ohio Valley during the months of February and March, 1884, was without precedent in the history of overflows throughout this vast district. Starting from the very source of the river the flood swept its entire length, spreading destruction on every hand and rendering thousands of people homeless and helpless. For the past three years the subject of overflows has received considerable attention and been generally discussed by the residents of the Ohio Valley, and several scientific theories have been advanced as to the cause for the increasing annual inundation throughout this valley. It is not my purpose to enter into the discussion of these various theories but to state briefly my views of the matter after a thorough analysis of the mass of literature touching upon the subject, placed at my disposal. What, then, is the cause or causes for these increasing annual overflows thoughout the Ohio Valley? Undoubtedly, to my mind, it is due to the removal of forests, the clearing of lands, and the introduction of the system of tile drains. It is hardly possible that these unprecedented overflows are caused by rainfalls, exceeding any heretofore known. One hundred years ago when the Ohio valley was lined with thick, dense forests, when land-clearing was in its infancy, and when tile drains were unknown, there were no such floods as have visited the Ohio during the past three years. The great forests which once flourished along the Ohio and its tributaries years ago, acted as absorbents themselves and also as creators and preservers of a soil which, sponge-like in itself, retained much of the water that now finds its way into the Ohio.

These forests are now being rapidly destroyed, and when this is done, particularly in the mountains and hilly regions, the soil washes away and the rains that were once absorbed through the ground, sweep down into the valley and thence into the river. At the very source of the Ohio these conditions are peculiarly prominent. The ranges of mountains on either side have been almost entirely stripped of their forests; the soil has been washed down to the strata of solid rock beneath, and the water from the melting snow and rains rush down their slopes a respectable deluge at the very beginning. As long then as the wholesale destruction of forests continues so long will the danger of increasing floods grow in proportion. It is a well known fact that years ago throughout Ohio, Indiana and Illinois, in those portions of the States that were woody and not hilly that during the winter months and well toward May, from one to six inches of water was held back by the accumulated leaves and twigs. All this is now changed by the removal of the timber, and especially by the clearing of the lands, the removal of drift and stone obstructions in creeks and the introduction of the principal factor in causing the floods, namely, tile drains or any other system of drainage calculated to remove water rapidly from any given point to another. The sub-draining of the wet lands with tile, which is constantly going on not only in Ohio, Indiana and Illinois, but in all other water sheds of the Ohio valley, in connection with the ditches, some as large as canals, necessary to better free the sudden rainfalls, all combine to carry the rain at once from the ground to the arteries. In mountainous, rocky and treeless regions a few hours rainfall will fill a parched gully with a dangerous torrent. The water makes its way to its final level as it would from a roof. There is nothing to impede it. With us a large proportion of a heavy rainfall is stowed in swamps, sloughs and woodlands. It seems certain that any agency that decreases the number or capacity of these natural reservoirs will increase the floods following an unusual fall of rain. In the valley of the Ohio where the over-flow during the late flood was the greatest there has been within the last few years, no marked increase in the acreage of land cleared of forests, so that if the increasing height of the flood is to be attributed to a modification of the natural condition, it is due to an increased area of drained lands, and the cause seems sufficient to produce the effect. Since 1876 fifty thousand miles of tile drain have been put down in Illinois alone, and it is believed that as much or more have been laid in Ohio and Indiana. The land in these States is generally level, abounding in wet lands and every foot of drain accelerates the journey of a portion of the rain that falls near it; and draining has but just begun. Every swamp and piece of wet land in the fertile regions of the country is destined to be drained, and the result is quite evident. It is very foolish to say we probably shall not have another flood. The probabilities, in truth, are all in the other direction. It is indeed, almost certain that great floods in the Ohio will be more numerous in the future than in the past. The record of the last few years is straight in line with such a conclusion, and science more than warrants it.

The people of the Ohio Valley ought to learn an important lesson from the experience of the last two years. They should recognize that similar, or even larger volumes of water will roll down this river annually and they should make suitable provisions accordingly. In closing my remarks upon the cause of the overflow I will state—that still greater floods may be looked for hereafter, and that many of the towns upon the banks of the Ohio will have to be abandoned for human habitation. The question will, without doubt, be asked what can be done to avert in a measure, this evil? My reply is, replace to a great extent the forests of the Ohio Valley. Construct large artificial reservoirs above Cincinnati, that will hold the excess of water till such a time as it may be used in improving navigation in the Ohio during the dry weather, or open a canal at a similar point that will rapidly carry the excess of water across the country into the Gulf of Mexico. These look like great undertakings, but I venture to say that one or the other of the methods will be adopted in a few years if these destructive overflows continue, and I see no reason why they will not. Again, the improvements of the Mississippi River that are now going on are also calculated to lessen in a degree the extent of these great overflows by allowing the water to find a ready exit below. There can be no doubt that the bed of the Ohio and Mississippi are quite similar in appearance, and if the contem-

plated changes in the bed of the Mississippi are also carried into
the Ohio it will necessarily lessen, or entirely remove, a minor
cause of these floods, namely, a retention or backing up of the
water by the sand bars or hills of sand in the bottom of these
rivers.   Honorable Robert S. Taylor, of Indiana, a member of
the Mississippi River Commission has very graphically placed
this matter before the public in an address delivered at St.
Louis, Missouri, by invitation of the Merchants' Exchange, on
January 26th, 1884, and afterwards published.   I will quote a
a few paragraphs from the article as appears on pages 10, 11
and 13 :

"If the Mississippi river could be emptied of its contents,
so as to expose its bottom dry and bare, the appearance
presented would be surprising to most of us.   Instead of a
comparatively level channel floor, corresponding in its general
features with the lands adjacent to the river, there would be
found a succession of great sand hills and intervening depressions.   Passing through one of these depressions, the observer
would find himself, it might be, a hundred and fifty feet below
the surface of the banks on either side.   Within a few thousand
feet he would encounter a sand hill, stretching across the channel, so steep that you could scarcely drive a horse up its
declivity, and perhaps a hundred feet high.   Having crossed
the top of this, he would descend into another basin, then climb
another hill, and so on.   When the channel is filled with water
the crests of these elevations approach the surface, and so con
stitute the bars so often mentioned in this connection.   In low
water the greatest depth above them is sometimes as little as
five feet, and often only six or seven.   This is insufficient for
profitable navigation upon a scale adequate to the growing demands of commerce.   To increase that depth is the improve-
ment desired."

"The effect of outlets upon the flood levels and upon the
river channel has been the theme of great controversy for a
generation past.   There is a class of aquatic doctors who regard
the Mississippi in every time of flood as sick, whose diagnosis
of the case is dropsy, and whose remedy is tapping.   Bills have
been introduced in Congress, and vigorously pushed, to provide
for the making of vast outlets by artificial means.   The oppo-

nents of such measures have claimed that the effect of such diminution of volume in the river is, to lessen its energy and transporting power, and so cause deposits of sediment, which choke up the channel, increase the flood heights, and thus make the last state of the river worse than its first. These views have been supported by many observed facts, and by what seemed to be unanswerable reasoning. Nevertheless, there has been felt by intelligent students of the question a strong desire for more facts, and for facts based on observations so made as to afford the highest possible guarantees of their accuracy. Some such facts we are now able to give.

" During the great flood of 1882, a number of crevasses occurred below Memphis. Less than three months prior to that time, a survey of that part of the river had been completed, so that we know its exact depth, width and cross section at those points as they were before the flood. After the flood a resurvey was ordered to be made in the locality of four of those crevasses, for the express purpose of ascertaining what change, if any, they had produced in the river channel. The results were as follows : at Malone's Landing, where the upper and least crevasse of the four occurred, there was a shoaling of the channel below the crevasse amounting to four per cent, of its cross section ; at Riverton there was a shoaling of fourteen per cent. ; at Bolivar, eleven per cent,; and at Mound Place, twenty-four per cent.

At Bonnet Carre, a few miles above New Orleans, a crevasse occurred a number of years ago, through which a large volume of water escaped into Lake Ponchartrain It remained open until the autumn of 1882, when it was closed. We had a survey of the river adjacent to this crevasse, made before its closure, and have just completed another made since. A comparison of the two shows that since the closure of the crevasse the channel space in the river below it has increased about twelve per cent. We have, therefore, in four cases, a filling up of the river bed following an outflow through a crevasse, and in one, a scouring out of the bed following the closure of a crevasse and the stoppage of its discharge. I am not now arguing the outlet question, and will not take time to comment on the sig-

2

nificance of these facts; but that they weigh more than a fools-
cap quire of conjecture, will be readily admitted."

It will therefore be seen that a deviation of the river from
its natural channel will accelerate deposits and assist in the
formation of bars or sand hills below, which will in turn impede
the waters in their onward course, and by filling up the river
bed becomes an agent in producing the floods. To obviate
this, these bars or hills must be removed, and that is one of the
duties imposed upon the Mississippi River Commission, of
which I shall not speak further in this connection.

The winter of 1883-4 was particularly severe throughout
the Ohio Valley. Large quantities of snow fell upon the mountains during the season, the temperature was remarkably low for
this latitude, in one instance reaching 22° below zero, Fahren-
heit thermometer, and the formation of ice was general from
the source of the Ohio to its mouth. With the Ohio Valley
covered by snow and ice, particularly in the upper portions, it
was not to be wondered that such a volume of water having an
easy egress as previously mentioned, came down the river
when the thaw commenced, especially so as it was accompanied
by a warm rain of nearly two weeks duration, extending over
this whole section of the country. While the river commenced
rising slowly at the headwaters about the first of February it did
not make any appreciable rise till assisted by the warm rains
which commenced falling on the fourth and continued almost
unceasingly till the fourteenth, inclusive. The following table,
accurately prepared for me at U. S. Signal Office, Washington,
D. C., will show the daily precipitation at the principal cities in
the Ohio Valley, during this period:

STATEMENT showing the precipitation, in inches and hundredths, at the below named places, from February 3d to 15th, 1884, inclusive, compiled from the records on file at the Office of the Chief Signal Officer of the Army.

DATE, 1884.	PRECIPITATION IN INCHES AND HUNDREDTHS.						
	Cairo, Illinois.	Cincinnati Ohio.	Evansville, Ind.	Louisville, Ky.	Paducah, Ky.	Pittsburgh, Pa.	Wheeling, W. Va
February 3............	0.00	0.00	0.00	0.00	0.00	0.00	0.00
" 4............	0.07	0.52	0.00	0.89	0.00	0.45	0.00
" 5............	1.17	1.71	0.50	2.38	0.00	0.76	0.32
" 6............	1.24	2.23	0.60	1.73	1.20	0.80	1.08
" 7............	0.18	0.33	1.50	0.63	0.30	0.34	0.62
" 8............	0.25	*.	0.27	0.00	0.00	0.01	0.00
" 9............	0.03	0.06	0.60	0.14	0.00	0.04	0.10
" 10............	0.51	0.00	0.00	0.61	0.30	0.13	0.00
" 11............	0.11	0.70	0.17	0.60	0.40	0.55	0.01
" 12............	0.13	0.07	0.30	0.27	0.00	0.06	0.52
" 13............	0.43	0.60	0.10	0.77	0.40	0.14	0.20
" 14............	0.00	0.60	0.47	*.	0.39	0.18	0.40
" 15............	0.00	0.00	0.00	0.00	0.00	*.	0.00

* Inappreciable.

SIGNAL OFFICE, WAR DEPARTMENT,
   WASHINGTON, March 10, 1884.

As early as the third of February it was clearly evident to all on the Lower Ohio that a great flood was coming, even greater than last year, and having been well warned and dearly taught by previous destructive floods to be on their guard in the future, the people, as best they could, made a general move from the bottoms to the hills and higher places with the most of their valuables. This timely move saved many lives and thousands of dollars worth of stock and other property which must certainly have otherwise been lost. The flood continued steadily, and on the fifth the river was reported as rising rapidly from Pittsburgh, Pa., to Cairo, Illinois.

Fortunately at this time the Mississippi was quite low, in fact being eight feet less than at the same period of the flood last year. The Tennessee, Cumberland and Wabash were also low as compared with the year before. This condition alone

saved the Lower Ohio from being visited by such a destructive
flood as occurred above, the river emptying itself rapidly into
the Mississippi and no backing up occurring from a rise in these
other rivers till the mass of water had passed down the Ohio,
and the danger therefrom was over. The river continued
rising, going beyond all former high water marks known in the
history of the valley, till the unprecedented heights given below
were reached. This table has been carefully prepared from the
records of the various local U. S. Signal Offices, and is the
standard measurement taken by the officer in charge from the
Government gauges at the height of the flood.

Pittsburgh, Pa.,	February 6th	1884.	33 feet	4 inches.
" Allegheny Riv.	6th	"	34 "	4 "
Wheeling, West Va.	" 7th	"	52 "	1 "
Cincinnati, Ohio,	" 14th	"	71 "	3¾ "
Louisville, Ky.,	" 15th	"	46 "	8 2-5 "
Evansville, Ind.,	" 20th	"	48 "	1¼ "
Paducah, Ky.,	" 22d	"	54 "	2¾ "
Cairo, Illinois,	" 23d	"	51 "	10 "

At Pittsburgh the water was thirteen feet four inches over
the danger line. At Cincinnati the water was four feet eight
and three-fourths inches higher than the highest water ever
before known there; and such is the proportional rise all the
way down till Cairo is reached where, from the following table it
will be seen that the flood of 1884 lacked four inches of being
as high as the highest point reached by any previous rise:

Cairo, Ills.,	February 26, 1882	51 feet	10¾ inches.
" " "	27, 1883	52 "	2 "
" " "	23, 1884	51 "	10 "

The weather during the flood was, at times, quite severe,
especially so about the time the water reached its highest point,
and several cases of freezing were reported. To add to the distress already existing, the entire valley was visited on February
19th by a most terrific gale, the wind at times reaching a
velocity of sixty miles an hour. The river, miles in width, was
thrown into a perfect sea, waves rolled into the submerged
cities and towns along its border from fifteen to twenty feet

high and spread destruction wherever they stuck. Many lives were lost and thousands of dollars worth of property destroyed. Many places would not have required aid had not this storm occurred. (For further reference to this storm see the log of the steamer Carrie Caldwell, page oo).

For reference I give below a table showing the highest stages of water in the Ohio from 1832 to 1884 inclusive, at the cities named.

AT EVANSVILLE.

Year.	Date.	Ft.	In.	Year.	Date.	Ft.	In.
1832	February	46	7	1877	January	41	5
1847	January	45	6	1880	February	42	10
1867	March	46	3	1882	February	44	9¼
1875	August	41	10	1883	February	47	9½
1876	January	43		1884	February	48	1¼

AT CINCINNATI.

Year	Date.	Ft.	In.	Year.	Date.	Ft.	In.
1832	February	64	8	1877	January	53	9
1847	December	63	7	1880	February	53	2
1867	March	55	8	1882	February	58	7
1875	August	55	4	1883	February	66	4
1876	January	51	9	1884	February	71	¾

AT PITTSBURGH.

Year.	Date.	Ft.	In.	Year.	Date.	Ft.	In.
1832	February	35	0	1877	January	23	7
1847	February	26	0	1880	February	22	0
1867	March	22	6	1882	January	21	9
1875	August	21	9	1883	February	27·	6
1876	September	23	3	1884	February	33	4

No one who did not see the river during the flood can form the slighest idea of the enormous mass of water that covered the country. In many places the river was from ten to fifteen miles wide. In three places it was thirty miles wide, while places of from three to five miles in width could be found anywhere. Never in the history of the Ohio River did such a large quantity of water pass Cincinnati during two months, as in the months of February and March, 1884.

The following are the figures of each day:

February	Ft.	In.	March.	Ft.	In.
1	32	7	1	25	5
2	40	5½	2	24	2
3	46	2	3	22	6
4	49	7	4	21	3
5	50	3	5	20	5
6	55	6½	6	19	4
7	60	4½	7	18	3
8	61	9½	8	17	11
9	62	10	9	24	..
10	63	..	10	30	8
11	65	1	11	36	10
12	66	10	12	39	10
13	68	8¼	13	47	3
14	69	11	14	48	4
15	71	0¾	15	48	3
2 A. M.	70	9¼	16	48	7
16	69	11	17	48	6
17	67	11½	18	49	8
18	65	6	19	48	8
19	62	9½	20	46	3
20	59	10	21	43	11
21	58	5	22	41	2
22	55	1½	23	40	9
23	51	5	24	40	11
24	47	10	25	41	9
25	44	8	26	41	3
26	40	10	27	40	2
27	35	11	28	38	10
28	32	11	29	38	8
29	28	4	30	38	3
			31	35	0

RELIEF MEASURES.

As soon as it became apparent that aid would be required for the unfortunates who had been driven from their homes by the high water, and in many instances lost their all, prompt and energetic measures were at once taken all over the country for their relief. The story has already been told, and all are familiar with the prompt and generous action of the general Government; the responses which came up from all over the land to the cry of distress from deluged communities, the free-will offerings from State Legislatures and City Councils, from churches, schools and lodges, wealthy corporations and private individuals, until the stream of supplies to relieve the distress of the unfortunates seemed hardly surpassed by the mighty stream of uncontrolled waters that caused it.

At Pittsburgh, Pa., the citizens formed a Relief Committee, chartered the towboat Iron City with a barge, and loaded it with supplies of food, bedding, fuel and clothing, valued at $5,000. This boat was placed in charge of the Secretary of the Citizens' Relief Committee, Rev. E. R. Donehoo, pastor of the Eighth Presbyterian Church of Pittsburgh, and on February 14th left Pittsburgh to render aid to the sufferers down the river. The following gentlemen were on board and assisted in the distribution of the supplies: W. H. Davis, of the Commercial Gazette, Charles F Jahan of the Dispatch, Robert W. Herbert, of the Post, Charles Wakefield, of the Leader, and Park L. Walter, of the Chronicle Telegraph. The boat distributed supplies as far as Parkersburg, West Virginia, then turning back reached Pittsburgh Feb. 20th. By direction of the Relief Committee a second trip was made to the relief of the sufferers leaving Pittsburgh the same day that the first returned, viz, February 20th. The boat was the steamer Resolute, with Captain R. C. Gray's model barge. It was loaded with $15,000 worth of supplies, being donations from Pittsburgh and the neighboring towns, consisting of food, clothing and bedding. Rev. E. R. Donehoo was again placed in charge with George R. Reppert and Joseph G. Siebeneck as assistants. The expedition went as far as Parkersburg, West Virginia and turned back as before, that being the limit to which their relief work extended. It would be next to impossible to describe all the relief movements connected with the recent flood in the Ohio, as accurate accounts of the same have not been kept, but suffice it to say that every city and town not submerged came nobly to the front with relief for the needy.

At Cincinnati the Relief Committee of the Chamber of Commerce took the matter actively in hand and worked with a good will. One hundred and eighty-four thousand dollars ($184,000) were raised and distributed; a large portion of which was used outside of Cincinnati. The steamer Granite State was chartered and did good service in distributing supplies above and below Cincinnati. At Louisville the Relief Committee distributed local supplies from skiffs, no relief boats other than Government boats being sent out.

INDIANAPOLIS BOARD OF TRADE.

The Indianapolis Board of Trade placed itself early in the field for the relief of the Ohio River flood sufferers by the organization of the Indianapolis Board of Trade Relief Committee with Mr. N. S. Byram as Chairman. Subscriptions and contributions were rapidly received, and on the 15th of February they chartered the steamer City of Frankfort, at Cincinnati, and took her to Madison, Indiana, where several car loads of supplies were awaiting distribution, by direction of the Relief Committee. The boat having been loaded with eighty thousand rations, six hundred bed comforts, and a full supply of medicines, she left Madison on the trip down the river on the morning of the 17th of February with Captain Jacob Remelin commanding under the direction of the Relief Committee. The following persons were on board during the trip which extended from Madison, Indiana, to Shawneetown, Illinois: Governor A. G. Porter, N. S. Byram, Chairman, W. P. Gallup, J. A. Closser, Eli Lilly, A. A. Barnes, R. O. Hawkins, D. M Ransdell. H. E. Frazer, Mayor McMasters, (Indianapolis), Dr. E. S. Elder, Secretary of State Board of Health, Dr. D. D. Waterman, Dr. J. B Dill, Mr. Will Fortune, for the Indianapolis Journal, Mr. W. Tindall, for the News and A. McMurray and Jesse Shoemaker for the Sentinel, all of Indianapolis.

Bruce Carr, Grand Master of the Masonic order in the State, accompanied the relief party, and distributed several hundred dollars, with more for the needy ones below.

Lieut. Delaney, U. S. A., accompanied the Frankfort as far as Evansville, by order of the War Department, and was among those who rendered most efficient service in relieving the sufferers during the trip.

The cost of the rations distributed was $6,825, and the entire cost of the trip, including the cost of the rations was $8,452   Rations were left at all the points needing them between Madison, Indiana, and Shawneetown, Illinois, while fifteen hundred were delivered to skiffs alone.   The expedition consumed eight days, the boat being discharged February 25th.

In addition to the regular army rations an additional ration of potatoes was issued in nearly every instance.   Two hundred and thirty dollars worth of medicines were also distributed. The Committee further gave relief by taking the steamer "Little Sandy," Captain Williams, commanding, with twelve thousand rations at a cost of $2,624, and going above Madison. The boat was chartered February 14th by the Indianapolis Board of Trade Relief Committee and left Madison on the 15th, was out two days, and returning the boat was discharged on the 17th.   W. P. Gallup and Col. Eli Lilly, of the Committee, with Alderman Rorison and Dr Garver, accompanied the expedition The expenses of the trip and boat were $127.   The Relief Com mittee kept in reserve a considerable sum of the relief funds and at a later date sent Messrs. Byram and Gallup to make a personal investigation of all damaged property from Lawrence-burgh, Indiana, down to the Illinois line.   This they did, nearly all the distance having to be made in skiffs, and forwarded their report to the Committee who sent to responsible parties, money in varying amounts to be used in rebuilding and repairing their houses, barns, fences, &c.

Below Evansville the worst state of affairs was found in Posey County, among the farming classes.   Between West Franklin and the mouth of the Wabash 107 houses were swept away or ruined by the flood, and between the mouth of the Wabash and the crossing of the L. & N. R. R. 36 more.   It is estimated that the owners of at least one-half of these houses will not be able to rebuild unless public assistance is extended them.   From Mt. Vernon to West Franklin Mr. Byram said he did not see a living thing, man or beast, nor a habitable house.   "It was a picture of desolation," said the gentleman, "such as no tongue or pen can describe."   The situation in the lower part of Vanderburgh County was found to be somewhat better, but bad enough.   Mr. Byram says that

3

through the losses among the farmers of this county do not aggregate as much as those of last year, the people are in even a worse situation than before, having lost their stock, farm implements and barns.

EVANSVILLE RELIEF COMMITTEE.

Evansville alone, of all the large cities throughout the Ohio Valley, can truly say that it was not damaged to the extent of one dollar by the recent flood except indirectly as businesss with the surrounding towns was interfered with. With the greatest flood ever known in the Ohio Valley, Evansville stood high and dry with several feet to spare. The great manufactories suffered no inconvenience, and were kept running full time and all business went on as though no such thing as a flood had ever been heard of. All these facts placed Evansville prominently before the country as the only city on the Lower Ohio which could be selected as headquarters for Government and private supplies for the relief of the sufferers. Boats were fitted out here for a sum considerably less than could have been done elsewhere, and the generosity expressed by the merchants toward all relief movements was quite marked. Immediately upon its being known that assistance would be required in the submerged districts neighboring to Evansville, a meeting of the citizens was held in the court house and the following Relief Committee at once appointed with power to act: Mayor T. C. Bridwell, Chairman; H. S. Bennett, W H. Caldwell, Dr. R. P. M. Ames, Charles Yeager, Treasurer, J. W. Lauer, Secretary, W. S. French, and John Albecker. Subscriptions were at once raised and the people responded nobly, several thousand dollars being collected the first afternoon. In this connection it is proper to state that the city, through its Mayor, T. C. Bridwell, gracefully declined the aid offered by Robert T. Lincoln, Secretary of War, from the fact that the city had not sustained any damage by the high water, and especially from the fact that we would be depriving other places actually in need. The following telegrams which passed between the officials will explain themselves.

TELEGRAM.
[Copy.]

WASHINGTON, D. C., February 13, 1884.

J. C. JEWELL, Collector of Customs,

Evansville, Indiana.

"Upon the suggestion of Senator Voorhees, I beg you to advise me what are the needs of your neighborhood for food and clothing to persons made destitute by the flood."

(Signed)   ROBERT T. LINCOLN,

Secretary of War.

To this Mr J. C. Jewell made the following reply.

TELEGRAM.
[Copy.]

EVANSVILLE, IND., Feb. 13, 1884.

HON. ROBERT T. LINCOLN, Secretary of War,

Washington, D. C.

"This neighborhood will need assistance. The water is still rising and the worst is not yet reached. The city is high and dry but the border above and below is inundated. The citizens are furnishing private relief."

(Signed)   J. C. JEWELL,

Collector of Customs.

TELEGRAM.
[Copy.]

WASHINGTON, D. C., Feb. 13, 1884,

THE MAYOR OF EVANSVILLE, IND.:

"You are authorized to purchase and distribute subsistence stores, clothing and other necessary articles to persons made destitute by floods, within your reach, to an amount not exceeding one thousand dollars Careful records of purchases should be kept to enable a Department officer to adjust the account when he can be sent. You will be expected to give the officer you receipt for stores, and account as agent of this Department for the distribution.   Please advise me by wire the number of destitute, and whether purchases can be made in your locality."

(Signed)   ROBERT T. LINCOLN,

Secretary of War.

In response to this Mayor T. C. Bridwell, after a thorough investigation and consultation with the Relief Committee, sent the following

TELEGRAM.

[Copy.]

EVANSVILLE, IND., Feb. 13, 1884.

HON ROBERT T. LINCOLN,

Secretary of War.

Washington, D. C.

"On behalf of our people I tender you their thanks for the proffered assistance. Evansville, happily, is above the reach of the flood and will not, for the present at least, require aid. All supplies are abundant here and can be readily purchased. The waters, however, are still rising and a large portion of two of our townships on the river are submerged. Aid for these may be required. I will at once confer with the officials of these townships and if aid is necessary will immediately advise you, and will cheerfully take charge of the relief tendered by you, and will distribute it in the manner indicated in your telegram of this date."

(Signed)   T. C. BRIDWELL,

Mayor City of Evansville.

TELEGRAM.

[Copy.]

WASHINGTON, D. C., Feb. 14, 1884.

HON. T. C. BRIDWELL, Mayor Evansville, Ind.

"I understand from your telegram of this date that you will not need the credit of $1000 offered you yesterday. If so please advise me as demands from other quarters are very pressing.

(Signed)   ROBERT T. LINCOLN,

Secretary of War.

To this dispatch Mayor Bridwell sent the following reply, which clearly voiced the sentiment of our citizens:

TELEGRAM.

(Copy.)

EVANSVILLE, IND., February 14, 1884.

HON. ROBERT T. LINCOLN, Secretary of War,

Washington, D. C.

"The people of Evansville and Vanderburgh County again decline the proffered aid. We can provide, not only for the suffering within our own borders, but are now preparing to assist other localities not so favorably situated as ourselves."

(Signed)   T. C. BRIDWELL,

· Mayor City of Evansville.

It will thus be seen that while at first thought aid would be necessary, after a careful consideration of the subject it was deemed not advisable to accept it as sufficient means were then in the hands of the Relief Committee to care for all the sufferers both above and below us, and properly within our district on either side of the river. On February 14th the Relief Committee chartered the steam tug Isabella and with a full supply of food, clothing and medicines, they descended the river into Union Township and rendered great relief to the farmers in the bottom lands. On the 15th a similar trip was again made down the river as far as West Franklin, and on the 16th the party ascended the river as far as Owensboro, Ky. On each trip rations were left with the parties relieved sufficient to last two weeks. Many found sick and helpless were brought to the city and placed in the hospitals, while hundreds of families who could not leave their homes were made comfortable by issuing to them a full supply of rations and medicines. Great credit is due the Evansville and Cairo Packet Company for the regularity with which they ran their boats during the flood. They were run at great risk and very often at considerable loss; but they were of immense service to the people in the submerged districts and it was to this that the company paid attention, these boats being the only means of communication that was offered the towns below Evansville and above Cairo. On February 20th, the day after the great storm that passed over the

Ohio Valley, the steamers Grace Morris and Isabella were chartered and two expeditions sent out to the aid of the sufferers. The Grace Morris went up stream with a portion of the Relief Committee, and Dr. Charles E. Lining, Health Officer, to look after the sick, while the Isabella went below with several other members of the committee, and at Henderson, Ky., took on board Dr. James Letcher. Both boats were out all day and rendered most valuable assistance to those who had been disabled by the storm. Several instances occurred where parties partially frozen or exhausted were taken from trees into which they had climbed the night before when their homes, already partially submerged, were swept away by the gale. As the water gradually subsided the plan of relief changed. The people had been fully supplied with food, but now came the time when clothing would be needed and assistance in replacing and repairing their homes required. The plan which was originally suggested by Governor Porter, of Indiana, was at this time generally adopted. This plan was as follows:

" I think that all moneys hereafter contributed for the relief of the flood sufferers should be applied to making habitable the dwellings of poor people who have suffered by the flood, and to the purchase of farming implements for needy people where the implements have been lost by barns or other places in which they were placed having been washed away. Sufficient money has been raised by the Relief Committees, and more than sufficient, along with the United States appropriation, for the purchase of food and clothing. Whatever surplus is left in the hands of relief committees should be applied to repairing and replacing dwellings and purchasing implements in such cases as I have named. The money used in this way last year was applied most usefully. It revived hope and courage, and stimulated industry. Since last year, working people whose houses were removed from their foundations and greatly damaged have not been able to accumulate means enough now to replace and repair them. Help given them will inspire them with new energy, and will, sooner than anything else, remove the necessity of any other kind of help. Every dollar in the hands of relief committees that can be thus used should be applied in this manner. Every dollar that has been sent to me will be applied in this manner, and I wish I had in my hands for that purpose many times as much as I have."

At this time also the Red Cross Association came actively to the front for now ha l the time arrived when this Association, of all others, could do the most good.

RED CROSS ASSOCIATION.

The Red Cross Association was organized for the relief of suffering by war, pestilence, famine, flood, fire and other calamities of sufficient magnitude to be considered national in extent. It operates under the provisions of the Geneva Treaty promulgated at Geneva, Switzerland, in 1864, and signed since then by all civilized nations of the earth; the United States giving its adhesion through President Arthur in March, 1882. Of the American Association President Arthur is the Chairman of the Board of Consultation. The Executive, consisting of Miss Clara Barton, President, Walter P. Philips, Secretary, George Kennan. Treasurer. The Trustees are Honorable Charles J. Folger, of New York. Secretary of the United States Treasury, Honorable Robert T. Lincoln, of Illinois, Secretary of War, and Honorable George B Loring, of Mississippi. The society is international in its character, non-partisan and non-sectarian in composition, discriminating in its judgment, unbiased in its action, grand in its aims, and efficient in its work. Through the instrumentality of the Red Cross Association much suff ring and destitution has been relieved throughout the Ohio Valley which it would have been almost impossible to reach but for this organization. With Miss Clara Barton at the head, and a large corps of active and intelligent assistants, the relief work performed by this Association has been most thorough and efficacious. Contributions of money and clothing have been sent to all points in the inundated districts of the Ohio Valley where such assistance was needed, while a thorough and careful investigation, by members of the Association, of the

flooded territory, has rendered the aid most beneficial. As soon
as it became apparent that the suffering from the high water
would necessitate the various relief movements, Miss Barton
removed her headquarters from Washington, D. C , to Cincinnati, Ohio, where she carefully and intelligently superintended
the distribution of a large amount of supplies donated from all
parts of the country, consisting of money, food, clothing and
fuel. As the water receded then came the time for the relief
proffered by this Association 'to be given. After remaining
several days in Cincinnati and relieving all the suffering so far as
it was met with, Miss Barton on March 3d, removed her headquarters to Evansville, Indiana, where arrangements were at
once commenced to reach and aid the sufferers between this
point and Cairo, Illinois. Captain J. V. Throop kindly placed
his steamer, the "Josh. V. Throop," at the disposal of the Red
Cross Society without any expense except the actual running
cost of the boat. The steamer was at once loaded with an
immense quantity of boxes, bales, barrels and bundles of clothing, being donations from various private parties and relief
organizations throughout the country which had been accumu-
lating here for some time, together with a large amount of bed
ding and fuel, and started on its mission of mercy down the
river in charge of Miss Clara Barton, Saturday, March 8th, 1884.
Miss Barton was accompanied and assisted on this trip by Dr.
J. B. Hubbell, of Washington, D. C., the Field Agent of the
Association, Rev. E. J Galvin, agent of the Chicago Red Cross
Association, Capt Coghill, agent of the St. Louis Association,
Miss Hamilton, of St. Louis, with Mrs. DeBruler and several
other Evansville ladies. Relief was given to all the sufferers
needing it between Evansville and Wickliff, Kentucky, below
Cairo. The party reached Cairo, March 15th, and after proceed-
ing down the river to Wickliff, Kentucky, turned back, arriving
at Evansville, March 20th. In addition to the supplies mentioned, the Rev. E. J. Galvin, of Chicago, had placed at his
disposal $25,000, from which checks were drawn and left
with any party needing financial assistance. Miss Barton and
her corps of assistants remained in Evansville after their return
until April 2d, when the relief transactions throughout the Ohio
Valley having been practically finished, she removed her head-

quarters to St. Louis, Mo., where a relief boat was at once fitted out and similar assistance tendered to the sufferers in the inundated districts of the Lower Mississippi. Miss Barton was further aided on this trip by Mr. John Hitz, of Washington, D. C*

GOVERNMENT RELIEF.
For the Ohio River Flood Sufferers.

On February 10th a meeting of the Congressmen from Ohio, Kentucky and West Virginia, presided over by Senator Sherman, was held in Washington to take steps to secure an immediate appropriation for the relief of the sufferers by the flood in the Ohio Valley. The necessity for such a meeting was quite apparent, and Congress, in response thereto, appropriated three hundred thousand dollars for such purpose on the following day. On February 15th, the first appropriation having been considered hardly sufficient to meet the demands, two hundred thousand dollars more were appropriated for the same purpose making five hundred thousand dollars in all to be expended under the direction of the War Department. The original plan of the Secretary of War, which was carried out, was to have one boat with supplies go down the river from Pittsburgh, two leave Cincinnati, one going up stream and the other down, one boat from Louisville to Evansville, and the fifth boat from Evansville to Cairo; but it was afterwards learned that additional boats would in some instances be required, and they were therefore sent out. Major S. T. Cushing of the Subsistence Department, was ordered to Pittsburgh in charge of the supplies, General Beckwith to Cincinnati, while Colonel Rufus Saxton took charge in Louisville Sixty thousand dollars were assigned to the relief of the flood sufferers between Pittsburgh and Ironton and more if needed. The steamer Katie Stockdale was chartered and left Pittsburgh for down the river with seventy-five thousand rations on board, in charge of Captain Rose, February 15th, the total value of the cargo exceeding twenty-five thousand dollars. From Cincinnati the steamer

*On May 25th Miss Barton made a second trip down the Ohio with the steamer "Josh V. Throop" under charter with household supplies and farming implements for the recent sufferers The boat went as far as Elizabethtown, or possibly a few miles below, and then turning back, proceeded up stream to Wheeling or Pittsburgh till the supplies were exhausted.

Granite State went up and the steamer General Pike came down, on February 17th, the latter only distributing about six thousand rations as far down as Taylorsport, Kentucky. The steamer Mattie Hayes left Louisville on February 15th in charge of Major E. B. Kirk, with seventy five thousand rations, arriving at Evansville February 18th, and turning back, reached Louisville February 24th. On all these trips rations were distributed on the return trip as well as on the one going out. The steamer Mattie Hayes made another trip on February 26th, leaving Louisville and going to Madison Indiana, and return. She carried on this trip fifty thousand rations and distributed thirty thousand. The remaining twenty thousand on her return to Louisville were placed on the steamer City of Frankfort together with eighty thousand purchased in Louisville, and another trip was made down the Ohio to Evansville leaving Louisville March 4th and arriving at Evansville March 9th. From Evansville some of these rations were sent by packet to Metropolis, Illinois. (See log of steamer Carrie Caldwell, second trip.) The steam tug "Osceola" was sent as a special boat from Louisville with seventy-five thousand rations, twenty thousand for Shawneetown, thirty thousand for Paducah and twenty-five thousand for other needy points. (See log of steamer Carrie Caldwell, first trip.) The steamer Carrie Caldwell made two trips from Evansville. On her first trip she left Evansville, Indiana, on February 17th with seventy-five thousand rations, going as far as Cairo, Illinois and returning. On her second trip she left Evansville, Indiana, March 5th, with one hundred thousand rations, going as far as Wickliff, Ky, on the Mississippi and returning. (See log of the two trips.) In addition to the above mentioned relief, aid was directly and indirectly furnished to the sufferers on the Upper Ohio as the emergency required, full reports of which have not yet been received, nor will they be published, unless Congress should call upon the Secretary of War for a full and detailed report of the same. Two hundred and twenty-five thousand dollars were expended above Madison, Indiana, and one hundred and twenty five thousand dollars between Madison and Cairo Illinois, while the remaining one hundred and twenty five thousand dollars were transferred to the relief of the Mississippi flood sufferers.

FIRST TRIP

OF THE

United States Relief Boat Carrie Caldwell,

TO AID THE

Ohio River Flood Sufferers:

Evansville, Indiana, to Cairo, Illinois

AND RETURN,

Febuary 17th to February 25th, 1884, inclusive.

Captain A. B. MacGowan, 12th U. S. Infantry, Commanding.

On February 15th, 1884, Captain A. B. MacGowan, 12th
U. S. Infantry in charge of the recruiting office at Louisville,
Kentucky, was detailed by Hon. Robert T. Lincoln, Secretary
of War, through Assistant Quartermaster General Rufus Saxton,
also of Louisville, to proceed to Evansville, Indiana, charter a
boat, purchase seventy-five thousand rations and go to the
relief of the flood sufferers between Evansville and Cairo.
With these instructions Captain MacGowan left Louisville at
once, arriving in Evansville on the morning of February 16th
and proceeded immediately to consult with Honorable William
Heilman for the necessary information relative to the chartering
of a steamboat and the purchase of supplies. By ten o'clock
in the forenoon the steamer Carrie Caldwell had been chartered,
bids received for the supplies and the contracts awarded. The
following, being the lowest bidders, received the contracts to
furnish the supplies :

George P. Heilman & Co.

480 sacks of meal @ $1 10	$514 80
38 bbls. hominy grits @ $2 50	110 20
Amount	$625 00

William Caldwell.

75 sacks @ 10c, 236¼ bush. Irish potatoes @ 45c. . . $113 81
63   "   @ 10c, 125   "   onions   @ 80c. . . 106 30
11208 pounds sugar @ 7c 784 56

Amount, ... $1,004 67

W. M. Akin & Son.

56250 pounds salt sides (769 pieces) @ 9¾c $5,484 37

Parsons & Scoville.

6006 pounds roasted coffee @ 17⅞c . . . . $ 1,073 58
17 boxes family soap, 1020 pounds . . . . . .
19   "   Atlantic   "   1140   "   . . . .
11   "   Olive   "   660   "   . . . .
2   "   Old reliable   120   "   . . . . . .
1   ".   Specialty   60   "   . . . . . .
                    3000 pounds soap @ 4c . .   120 00
211 barrels flour @ $5 00 . . . .   1,055 00
2323 pounds baking powder @ 10c 232 30

Amount, ... $2,480 88

As soon as the contracts were awarded no time was lost in
placing the supplies upon the boat, and by ten o'clock in the
evening the Carrie Caldwell was fully equipped and ready for
an early start in the morning. A full supply of medicines and
disinfectants, were also procured for distribution among the
sick along the route, and by special direction of the Secretary
of the Treasury I accompanied the expedition in charge of the
medical department, to attend to the sick, and issue medicines
when needed. Much credit is due Mr. William Caldwell, of
whom the boat was chartered, for his personal supervision in
furnishing the boat with an abundantly well filled larder and
sparing no pains to see that everything was made comfortable
for us upon the trip. Mayor T. C. Bridwell, of Evansville,
kindly consented to accompany us, and from his thorough
knowledge of the people and country below here rendered to
Captain MacGowan most valuable aid in assisting him in the
distribution of the supplies.

Everything then being in readiness we left Evansville on
our first trip down the river with Government rations for the

Ohio River flood sufferers, on Sunday morning, February 17th, 1884, with the following officials on board.

Capt. A. B. MacGowan, 12th U. S. Infantry, commanding.

Dr. R. P. M. Ames, Assistant Surgeon of the U. S Marine Hospital Service, in charge of the Medical Department.

Mayor T. C. Bridwell, of Evansville.

John Weed, Captain of steamer Carrie Caldwell.

J. F. Crane, Mate   "   "   "

Henry Matheny, Pilot   "   "   "

John Orr, Engineer   "   "   "

Eugene Brady, 1st Clerk   "   "   "

George Swearanger, 2d Clerk "   "   "

Edward Lamb, Steward   "   "   "

The following is the revised log as kept by me on the trip:

"The first stop was at Barker's and Sanders', just above Henderson, Indiana shore. People all right and no supplies were left.

The second stop was at Henderson. Capt. MacGowan, Mayor Bridwell and myself went ashore and consulted with ex-Mayor Peters, F. E. Kriepe and Thomas L. Cannon. Said parties stated they were all right in Henderson and could care for all the sufferers that had come to them. Three hundred bags (paper) were purchased, and two flour scoops. No supplies were left.

WEST FRANKLIN, IND.

Arrived at 2 p m. Left rations for fifty people, 500 rations. All the houses but four have water up to the second story. Hays' store is under water to the roof. Supplies were left with Postmaster Seitz. Mrs. Barbie H. Rossman was found sick with pneumonia, and I left medicine. She is 56 years old. Her daughter-in-law Francis was sick with conjestive malaria, and medicine was left.

At Mr. John Oliver's place his mother was sick with pneumonia and dysentery. One woman just gave birth to a child. Mrs. Grimp's child was sick with malaria, and Mary E. Duncan with dysentery. No distress on the Kentucky shore opposite West Franklin. At widow Weaver's house on Mt. Nebolt, the water is just up to the door. Diamond Island is all covered. Bement's corn cribs, with 45,000 bushels, are dry; his pens, with 2,500 bushels are also dry. Alzey, Ky., is all gone but the store and Postoffice, and no one is living in the place. The store was owned by Cooper & Co. The New York store is in about twenty feet of water.

MT. VERNON, IND.

Arrived at 4 p. m. Captain MacGowan, Mayor Bridwell and myself went ashore and met the following Committee on Relief for the sufferers:

E. Smith, Mayor, President; J B Gardner. J. P. Welbourn, John Pfeffer, S. Millner, Treasurers, J. D. Dieterlie, Secretary, Alfred D. Owen and William Spillman.

It was found that a number of flood sufferers were in a bad condition, but the committee had done excellent work. Rations for five hundred people were left. The boat remained at Mt. Vernon all night and left for below at 6 a, m.

UNIONTOWN, KY.

February 18, arrived at 8 a. m. The town is in a terrible condition, every house, of which there are about 700, are all in water from the second story to the roof Only four are dry and they are back of the town on the hill. All business except for the necessaries of life, has stopped, and what little there is done is from the second floor through the windows into boats. Boats take the place of all teams, &c., as the water is from ten to twenty feet deep over the town. Plank sidewalks are floating on a level with the second stories. No houses have been moved from their foundations as yet. The river rose three and a half inches here last night (Sunday). There is no telegraphic communication at all, and it is hardly probable that the telephone can be used as the office is all under water. Captain J. K. Freeman, P. M. has moved his office to the second floor and mail is delivered by boats. A one-story house passed down from above while we were here. The churches are all under water, the Methodist being the most so, as the water is at the top of a lamp post in front of the church. The Baptist Church has water over the pews. On Second Street the water is on the roof of J. R. Warren & Co.'s store. The town is about one-half mile wide and two miles long. The Commercial and

Grand Hotels are in water to the second floor. The water is now three inches lower than last year and still rising rapidly. Locals say it will be half a foot higher than last year. On arriving the following Relief Committee was met by Capt. MacGowan, Mayor Bridwell and myself: J. C. Hamilton, C. D. Mattingly, George Gillicrep, W. T. Cannon, John Cartmell, W. T. Taylor (City Marshal) and T. H Champman. They stated that the mass of the people in the town were dependent upon the factories and business houses for support, and as these were closed and they could not get their daily pay they were in want. About 500 families are needy, and a large territory on the Indiana and Kentucky shores, about twenty-five or thirty miles back, being flooded, depended upon Uniontown for support. Rations for 1,000 people were left (10,000 in all). River here twenty-five miles wide. Left at 10 a. m.

After leaving Uniontown we found John Castella's house with chimney floating down the river four miles below, it came from Mackey's plantation Parties were in a skiff and had removed a rocking horse, chairs, beading, etc., from the garret. Indian Mound was only a few feet out of water and a house lodged on it. The mouth of the Wabash is a perfect sea. Slack's Landing is twenty feet under water and no one there.

SHAWNEETOWN, ILL.

Arrived at 11 a m. We met Mayor Millspaugh, Mr. Carroll and others. No Relief Committee has been organized here, yet the Mayor stated that there were about 1,500 people in the town and near country that would need relief—some from Kentucky and some from the hills back of town where they had gone for safety. Fifteen thousand rations were left for distribution. The town is completely submerged and the destitution is great. Old pork houses, factories and mills are filled with men, women and children, white and colored, all driven from their homes and the latter destroyed.

While the rations were being placed upon the wharf-boat Captain MacGowan, Mayor Bridwell and myself accepted the kind invitation of John Nicholson to show us the most interesting portion of the submerged town. Shawneetown is a place of about two thousand inhabitants and the majority of the popu·

lace are quite poor, depending upon the mills and factories for their support. As soon as it became known that the vast amount of water from above would place the river far above the level of the levee it was decided for the safety of the town to cut the levee and let the water come in gradually rather than risk the breaking of the levee when the river would be at an extreme height and the water pouring in would cause immense destruction to property. The levee was accordingly cut and the rise of water in the town, proper, a gradual one. The residents have moved back into the hills, one and a half miles distant, or gone to the neighboring towns of Enfield, F quality, Mt. Vernon and Eldorado. Railroad and telegraphic communication is entirely cut off but the latter will be resumed in a few days. The weather has been intensely cold for the past few days and the suffering is great. The town is submerged to the depth of ten to thirty feet, and in some places the current reaches a velocity of ten miles an hour. In skiffs we traversed the town and saw destruction on all sides. Hundreds of houses are entirely under water and many are swept away or completely demolished. Only the three story buildings have their roofs out of water. All the high, available buildings are filled with refugees, such as mills, factories and school houses.

In twenty feet of water, back of the city, the porkhouse was found to be a large building three stories high. One portion is of brick, but it was built forty years ago and is now crumbling into ruins. The main portion is built of large and heavy timbers and may be a reliable refuge, but it hardly looks it now. The people who have gathered there are among the poorest in the city. There are forty-five persons, whites and blacks, quartered there, few of whom are in the best of health and two are bed-ridden. The place is large and roomy inside, and the roof of the lower portion affords an excellent promenade. Altogether the porkhouse is better suited to its present uses from the standpoint of convenience than any other retreat of the sunken city. The water flows through the windows at a proper depth to admit an oarsman seated in a skiff without knocking off his hat. Two broad stairways lead up to the third or habitable floor above. A few of the smaller divisions apportioned to families presented an inviting appearance, but the general surroundings were filthy and squallid in the extreme, and much sickness and disease must emanate therefrom.

ON THE HILL.

A mile away on the hill 118 more unfortunates are biding the fall of the waters. Most of these are lodged in the army tents pitched on the slopes of the hill, some within view of the town and some hidden by the crown of the hill. Here were also encountered squalor and sickness, the latter arising from the exposure and the unhealthy food.

Near the same place are several families in cabin-covered flatboats. One of these is a widow whose husband occupied a sick bed when the water first began to climb the outside of the levee. He was seized with a delerium in which he died. The unhappy widow and her three little ones were relieved from their sad situation through the generosity of a private citizen, who furnished the funds for the burial and tendered the family the use of the flatboat during the highwater season.

On our return we met a funeral in boats going to the cemetery on the hills, back of the town.

Just before leaving, Mr. B. F. Trumbull, of Raleigh, Ky., reported one hundred people suffering in the hills back of Raleigh, mostly colored, some white. One thousand rations were therefore issued to them and left at Shawneetown to be delivered. After remaining three hours at Shawneetown we resumed our journey down the river.

BLACKBURN, KY.,

opposite Shawneetown, the water is all over the place. Mr. J. C. Bunch, Postmaster, has all the goods of the place on two barges in front of the store in which he and his family are living.

SHOTWELL COAL MINES.

The village is all under water and the people have gone away. No relief could be given.

CASEYVILLE, KY.

Arrived at 4 p. m. Left at 4:30 p. m. There were two funerals yesterday and one to-day in boats. The place is all under water with the exception of a few houses back of the town

5

on the bluff.   The water stands seven inches less than last year.
We met Capt. D. A. Brooks, Postmaster, who stated that there
was no absolute suffering, only bother, and no assistance was
needed; therefore they had not formed a relief committee.
They had been offered State relief, but refused it for the time
being.   The water is twelve feet deep in the streets.   The town
prison and Presbyterian Church are full of water.   On account
of the strong wind it was not safe to proceed farther that night,
we therefore crossed the river to the Illinois side where, under
the shelter of a high bluff, we remained all night.   During
the evening Dr. Barkley, with a party, came to us in skiffs and
stated that in the rear of the town there were about one hundred
people needy, of whom Postmaster Brooks had not known.
We therefore visited Caseyville again in the morning and left
one thousand rations.

WESTON, KY.

Arrived February 19th, 1884, at 7 a. m.   The town is
in ten feet of water and all the houses, twenty-five in number,
are submerged.   Mr. Lamb and others stated that while every
one was comfortable, they had a few poor people on the hills,
but not needy. . Aid was offered, but they did not require it.

FORD'S FERRY, KY.

The town is composed of about six good houses, which are
all under water.   The wharf-boat was pulled to a point one-
fourth of a mile above the place and tied to a tree.   They
did not need any assistance.

CAVE-IN-ROCK, ILL.

Only a few families are suffering, but some from Saline
are in a bad condition, and 1,000 rations were left.   We took
a skiff and rowed into the cave to the extreme end.   The cave
is 40 feet wide, 200 feet deep, and about 8 feet above our heads.
The water is at last year's high water mark.

ELIZABETHTOWN, ILL.

One-fourth of this place is under water.   Mr. McAmis,
Postmaster, said no relief was needed, and had heard of no
complaints; therefore no supplies were left.

ROSE CLARE, ILL.

The town is all under water. It has a population of 4,000 and about seventy-five houses. No relief committee has been formed. All the people are out of employment and are back on the hills. The river is five inches higher than last year, with only three houses dry. John Hogan and family of five were all found sick. John Hogan, pneumonia; Maggie Hogan, typho malarial fever; Katie Hogan, congestive fever. The above family is in the house of J. F. Durkin. Mrs. Mary Ledynski, widow of the late Dr. Ledynski, was found sick with chills and fever. I visited all and left medicines and directions. There are no physicians in the place, and these people have been sick for a week. Two thousand rations were left with William Davis for distribution.

CARRSVILLE, KY.

Population, 250—75 houses. Only five families were compelled to leave their houses. River seven inches above that of last year. One hundred people were suffering in the immediate vicinity, and 1,000 rations were left with R. A. Croster.

PARKINSON'S LANDING.

No provisions left—all right. River 3 inches higher than last year, and still rising.

GOLCONDA, ILL.

Arrived at 3 p. m. Population, 1,200. One half of the town is flooded, and the water one foot above that of last year. There is fifteen feet of water in the streets, with two inches over the second floors. The town is entirely surrounded, and the only means of exit is by a footpath to the hills at the south of the town. The mills, factories and stores are all closed, and many people are homeless and without food. All the sufferers are taken care of by the people to the best of their advantages. The citizens have responded well. The Relief Committee consisting of Major A. D. Pierce, J. C. Baker, and Mayor Theodore Steyer stated that all assistance was worthy and would be fully appreciated. The people are coming in from the bottoms, with about six families from Kentucky. There are at least 550 worthy people, and more coming. Ten thousand rations were left. A heavy fog, followed by a violent gale, prevented our leaving Golconda till Wednesday morning. During the gale the "Caldwell" parted three large hawsers at once, and swinging around broke a hole in her roof and staging. Captain Mac-Gowan while trying to reach the boat in a barge, narrowly escaped being blown into the river. The barge was captured by skiffs and towed to the wharf boat. Trees were blown down, and but for the fact that the wind was off shore many houses would have been ruined and lost. The damage elsewhere must be great.

BAY CITY, ILL.

Arrived February 20th, 1884, at 7 a. m. Ten houses is the size of this place. The warehouse is two feet out of water. Only one family have been drowned out and they are taken care of.

BIRDSVILLE, KY.

Is half under water. Met R. M. Johnson, Postmaster. Three families are drowned out, but all are cared for. No relief left.

SMITHLAND, KY.

Arrived at 9 a. m. This town, of about 600 is entirely under water, the river being two and a half feet higher than last year and still rising. The gale of last night has destroyed thousands of dollars worth of property; $20,000 will not replace it. The wind was on shore and did immense damage to the front of the town, not a sound house now being on Front Street. W. Ellis' large store-house, back of the Planters' Hotel, is a complete wreck, while the river is full of floating household goods and furniture of all kinds. Thirty houses were swept away last night and three-fourths of the people are destitute. There is not enough bread in the town to last them two days. The town is flooded back to the hills, being fifteen to twenty feet deep in the streets. As Captain Ceister says, "the storm has ruined us." The only brick house standing is the Court House. No relief committee has been formed. Mr. Hewitt, representing the State of Kentucky, is here. He has left $500, to be distributed among fifty families, with four gentlemen—Mr. Hendrich, Judge Gibson (Police Judge), Mr. Grayot and Mr. Adams. Mr. Hewitt was going up the river on the Kentucky side, but when told that we had relieved all above, he returned to Paducah, from whence he came, with us, to await further instructions from the Governor. Shawneetown was truly deplorable, but this place is worse. Captain MacGowan wishes to express his sincere thanks to Mayor Bridwell and myself, for the valuable aid rendered him in distributing the supplies and assigning the amounts to the different ports. Sickness has been abundant and medical services have been in constant demand. Four thousand rations were left at Smithland. We expect to part with Mayor Bridwell at Paducah, as home work calls him. He has been uneasy to get back, but could not before reaching Paducah as it is impossible for trains to run owing to the high water, and the steamboats are quite irregular.

NEW LIBERTY, ILL.

Arrived at 12, noon. The entire town is in twenty feet of water. There were fifty houses in the town and thirty were swept away in the gale last night. The suffering is terrible and the destitution great. From here to Paducah, Ky , the entire country is covered with from twenty to thirty feet of water. Supplies were left with Captain Jacobs at Hambletsburg, two miles above, as we could not land at New Liberty. Six thousand rations were left for 600 people. The river is two and a half feet higher than last year. There are hills on both sides of the river, which is one and a half miles wide at this point.

ALIDA POINT, ILL.,

Four miles above Paducah, three houses and several barns were washed away by the gale last night. Some of them lodged two miles below in the woods.

PADUCAH, KY.

February 20, 1884—Arrived at 2 p. m. The city, with the exception of a few squares, is completely under water from three to ten feet in depth. Great damage has been done by the gale of last night, and the people are in a most distressing condition. No landing could be made at the wharf boat for fear of injuring the adjoining buildings, and we had to go to the rolling mills above the city to make a landing. The Gus,

Fowler, Henry Tyler and Silver Cloud were laid up there. In a row boat Captain MacGowan, Mayor Bridwell and myself entered the city, going down Locust Street, which had five feet of water in it. Yeaser's drug store, the Southern Hotel and Presbyterian Church on Locust Street, have water on the first floor. The "News" office has about two feet on the first floor. Rowing down Broadway we went to the Richmond House. All of Broadway has water up to the first floors back to Oak Street. The American National Bank has moved up stairs.

Arriving at the Richmond House we rowed into the office and there met the Relief Committee and Mayor Charles Reed. Their story of the suffering and destitution was terrible. No less than 3,000 people are destitute in and around the city. They are worthy of all the aid they can get.

Paducah has received $1,000 from the State, but that is only a drop in the bucket. Paducah is truly a Venice.

The only boats running are those of the Evansville and Cairo Packet Company, and they deserve great praise for so nobly keeping up their trips. The Hopkins and Dexter are running through to Cairo, as the Gus. Fowler is disabled. During the gale last night, one house, with a man, woman and two children went adrift, and all were lost. The gale was beyond description, the waves rolling into the city about fifteen feet high, and reached the second story of the Richmond House. This exceeds anything in the memory of the oldest inhabitants, and as the Postmaster (Mr. Ashcraft) said, it equalled any storm he had ever seen on Cape Hatteras. Buckman & Brann's large tobacco warehouse was destroyed and 300 hhds of tobacco were lost. The wind blew the waves rightnt oo the shore. The river is three feet higher than last year and still rising. In the First Ward alone 550 people are distitute. The Relief Committee consists of, first the Central Committee, composed of Mayor Charles Reed and J. L. Bethsharer, County Judge, then the General Committee, consisting of one man from each ward as follows, six in all :

First Ward, M. Weil; Second Ward, George Rogers; Third Ward, J. W. Fisher; Fourth Ward, J. R. Smith; Fifth Ward, William Clark; Sixth Ward, W. E. Augustus. On arriving at Paducah we had about 18,000 rations left.

Seeing the great necessity of aid, Capt. MacGowan telegraphed for 40,000 rations for Paducah. We retained our rations for points below and will supply Paducah with 40,000 rations on our return. Mayor Bridwell left us at Paducah and will return to Evansville as soon as possible. But for the gale Paducah would not have needed any assistance.

METROPOLIS, ILL.

Arrived at 4:30 p. m. The town is half under water, and the destruction of property by last night's gale is terrible. The pen can not describe it. Four or five acres that are overflowed are one mass of wrecked and broken houses and buildings all drifted in together.

We were not able to land at the wharf-boat and went into a cove one mile above the city. During the gale last night the waves rolled into the city fifteen feet high and spread destruction wherever they struck. Twenty buildings were swept away and one hundred entirely demolished Seventy-five or eighty-five thousand dollars will hardly cover the loss. Among the houses destroyed are the McCorley Hotel, Mrs. Green's house and J. C. Willis' old warehouse. J. C. Willis, while endeavoring to save some property on the wharf-boat, had his thigh broken by being thrown against the side of the boat by the waves. The water beats the high water mark of 1867 by two feet. The town has twenty acres under water, and has a population of 4,000. Not a building is left sound on Front Street. The principal men that have given to the flood sufferers are the chief losers. Four or five thousand dollars each is the rule. They would not have asked for any aid if the gale had not occurred. The large stave factory of Shelton & Meyre is completely destroyed. One hundred families are without food or homes, five hundred persons in all. Five thousand rations were left. The Relief Committee consists of Mayor J. H. Norris, F. C. Obermach and T. S. Stone. The Committee took the steamer Massac with Captain MacGowan and myself, and ran up to the Caldwell one mile above town, and loaded her with the supplies.

Yost, Bigelow & Co.'s large spoke factory, employing 300 men, is greatly damaged, and the men are thrown out of employment. A large quantity of lumber was lost last night, and

the four saw mills belonging to Wm. Twole & Co. have quit
running till the water recedes. The flour mill of Quantee Bro.
with a capacity of 300 bbls a day has been greatly damaged and
shut down. All other mills, factories, stores, &c., are closed,
and the people are busy trying to save what little'there is left.
After unloading supplies we remained in the cove all night.

JOPPA, ILL.

February 21st, 1884.—Arrived at 6:45 a. m. The town
had about twenty-five houses before the gale of Tuesday. All
the houses are flooded except two or three back on the hills.
Copeland's store and adjacent buildings are flooded to the
second story. During Tuesday's gale the waves ran fifteen feet
high and completely destroyed seven houses and wrecked five
more. Copeland's store was considerably damaged. He has
all his household goods on a barge in front of the store. The
gale began at 2 p. m. and lasted till midnight. Many persons
have lost their all, not even a change of clothing being left. Mrs.
Brinton, who owned two houses on Front Street, lost both of
them and has not a cent left. The suffering is terrible. W. T.
Thompson, Postmaster says $4,000 will just about cover the loss
on property and $2,000 on household goods. Rations for fifty
people (500) were left with Mr. Thompson for distribution
among the sufferers.

OGDEN'S LANDING, KY.

This place was comprised of one large two story house,
warehouse and store. These the property of the Ogden family,
were all swept away in Tuesday's gale. The whole site is under
twenty feet of water. No landing was made. Not a soul left
there.

CALEDONIA, ILL.

Arrived at 8 a. m. Here we found two houses in which
were living five families from Kentucky; Rolus Woodfall was
sick with chills and fever, Tom. Woodfall, pneumonia. Medicines and instructions were left for them. There are eight
people in all at the upper landing. During the gale Tuesday,
the waves rolled into this place fifteen feet high, completely
destroying John Mohr's grist mill and drowning two cows. No

supplies for Caledonia were needed.   At the lower landing we met Mr. Worthington, light house keeper.   Nearly all the sufferers are from Kentucky, as the Illinois side is a bluff high and dry.   Kentucky opposite is all under water for three miles. People comfortable with plenty to eat.

At the lower landing at Caledonia the Government light has just ground enough to stand on. *

MOUND CITY

Is dry.   There are bulk heads all around the river front made of sand, gravel and planks.   Tuesday's gale was off shore and not much damage was done.   The river is six feet higher than the level of the town.

We met the Mayor, George Meitz, and the following coun-cilmen: Q. A. McCracken, C. M. Bell, J. W. Real, and Mr. Myre.   They stated that no relief was needed.   All the mills, factories, and even the marine ways are running and no one is out of employment, and all comfortable.   We left for Cairo at 10:30.

Halliday's large house on the Kentucky side, just above Cairo, was completely destroyed by the gale.

CAIRO.

Arrived at 2 p. m., February 21st, 1884.   There are bulk-heads for aboutten squaresin front of the city.   We will take coal here and remain all night.   The city is comparatively dry.   The levee has been raised since last year, except the distance stated. No relief is needed at Cairo.   We met Mayor Halliday and others.   The river is 51.9 on the gauge.   The levee is in an excellent condition.   The Mississippi levee is 56 feet high and 5 feet out of water.   The Ohio levee is 55 feet high with 3 feet extra bulkhead. The Ohio levee is 90 feet wide with a slope of 1 to 5 on the outside.   The Mississippi levee is 20 feet wide with a slope of 1 to 7 outside and 1 to 2 on the inside.

THE RETURN TRIP.

February 22, 1884.—Last evening while taking on coal a report was sent to Capt. MacGowan that Bird's Point, opposite

---

* The entire damage to Government lights on the Ohio River, between Cincinnati and Pittsburgh by the recent flood will not exceed $400   Only six of the 208 lights were destroyed by the water, thirty being entirely swept away.   Between Cincinnati and Cairo there were 211 lamps, and it is estimated that at least one-third of that number were entirely displaced.

Cairo, on the Missouri shore, had suffered terribly by Tuesday's gale, and needed assistance.   Investigation showed that fifteen houses were washed away and that the whole place was under water, and great destitution.   The people had received aid from Cairo, but seeing the great necessity for immediate and substantial relief, and as the St. Louis relief boat had not been heard from, though out of our jurisdiction, Captain MacGowan transferred to a steam tug kindly furnished by Mayor Halliday, 5,000 rations, and sent the tug to their relief, Dr. John A. Benson, of the U. S. Marine Hospital Service, being in charge.

We left Cairo at 6:20 a. m. February 22.   Tom Merriwether and another party, with two negroes, while attempting to cross the river opposite Mound City, on Tuesday, were caught in the gale and all lost.   The river has a terrible current here.   Old river men say they never saw anything like it before. At Cairo it is seven miles an hour.   The average is at least five miles an hour.

TERRELL'S LANDING, KY.,

Is all gone.   Three houses and one warehouse comprised the place, and were all swept away in Tuesday's gale.   Robert Merriwether's house is gone, but the chimney is left standing. All along the river the woods are full of broken houses, quarters and halfs, and all kinds of household goods and furniture.   The loss is frightful.   We are averaging five miles an hour going up stream, the current being very strong.   Several rafts of logs have been seen with wagons and farming implements upon them.

MARSHALL'S LANDING, KY.

The warehouse is still standing, and the water is up to the eaves.   Same at Chandt's landing.

TURNER'S POINT, KY.,

Opposite Caledonia, we found a terrific current, at least ten miles an hour.   We just moved in going against it.   This point is owned by Judge H. T. Turner, of Henderson.

BROOKLYN, ILL.

Arrived at 2 p. m., February 22d, 1884.   The town, a quarter of a mile wide and a mile and a half long, is all under water. During Tuesday's gale thirteen houses were entirely swept away and ten greatly damaged. The waves were ten feet high. Some portions of the town are dry. The store of Steele & Son has a bulkhead in front and is dry. Two school-houses are full of people, about thirty in all. The Daly's grist and saw mill is a total wreck. Household and farming implements are floating around the town. Several brick houses have crumbled. The town originally had sixty houses and a population of 200. H. D Hall lost his house, coopershop and all he owned including $200 in cash, which was in the house. All but one of Wm. Allen's tenement houses are gone. The Postmaster, T. B. Alexander, and Dr. J. D. Young stated that the suffering was great and that aid had been needed for three days. The people came from back in the country as far as Stringtown. It was estimated that at least 500 people were needy and 5,000 rations were left to be equally divided between Brooklyn and Stringtown.. A very sad incident was the death yesterday of Mrs. Sallie Tanner's child. Having lost everything and having no means, she obtained from Mr. Alexander, a cracker box in which to bury her child. Much sickness was found. River four feet higher than last year and still rising. The town was never before flooded. Alexander's store is filled with people from below. The school house for white children has seven families in it, and the one for colored children contains twenty families. Left at 3 p. m. for Paducah.

PADUCAH, KY.

Arrived at 4 p. m. and landed two miles above the city John Allard's house, in Illinois, opposite, has water up to the eaves. The old Government Barracks, below the city, are under water. On arriving at Paducah, Captain MacGowan received the following telegram, as did also Mayor Reed, from Rufus Saxton, Assistant Quartermaster General, at Louisville, in reply to his of the 20th, asking for 40,000 extra rations : ''Purchase 10,000 rations for Paducah. I will send 30,000 more from here at once.''

Under this authority the following supplies were purchased from the lowest bidders:

Ed. P. Noble & Co., 7,500 lbs. bacon, @12c . . . . **$** 900 00
City Flouring Mills Company, 57 bbls flour at $4 . . 228 00
J. R. Smith & Co—
 200 lbs. coffee at 12½c 25 00
 300 lbs. coffee at 17½c 52 50
 750 lbs. sugar at 6½c 48 50
 500 lbs. rice at 6c 30 00
J. K. Bondman & Co—
 300 lbs. coffee at 17½c 52 50
 750 lbs. sugar at 6½c 48 75
 500 lbs. rice at 6c 30 00
                 ————
Total $1,415 25

The actual cost per ration was 14 cents. The actual cost per ration purchased in Evansville was 9 cents.

This amount will be distributed by the Relief Committee by orders on the firms of whom the purchases were made, until the extra 30,000 rations arrive from Louisville. The river stands at 54 3-10 and rising slowly; one foot higher than when we were here on the 20th. Paducah is to-day feeding 3,000 people, and by another week it is estimated that 5,000 will have to be fed. On this trip Captain MacGowan has distributed near 90,000 rations and the entire cost, including the boat, will amount to nine rations for $1, or $9,567 75. As locomotion is performed only by boats, parties having them are charging exorbitant prices to row people from place to place. One person paid $7 to go in a boat to his train and $6 for his railroad ticket after getting there. A large number of railroad men (negroes) were paid off yesterday, and being drunk, they are causing great disturbance and riots are feared. Plundering is great. Last night, by force, they took charge of the colored church (Baptist.) They were run out to-day by the police. The State Guards were called out with head quarters at the Custom House. All is peaceful and quiet to-day. There are 4 feet 8 inches of water in the cellar of the Custom House. We were treated to a view of the city from the cupola of the Custom House by Major Ashcraft, Postmaster. As far as the eye can

reach there is nothing but water. Passengers of the C. O. &
S. W. Railroad have to be transferred by boat six miles out on
the road to Bond's Station. We remained here all night and
left Paducah at 6:30 a. m. February 23d. At Dr. Fisher's, just
below New Liberty, the steamer Metropolis was rescuing three
persons from the roof of a floating house. Just below New
Liberty, about a mile, are fifteen houses scattered along in the
woods, all washed away from New Liberty during the gale.
The steamer E. Lewis was repairing there and is now a total
wreck, parts of the boat being seen for miles below New Liberty.
Back of New Liberty the grave yard is all under water. The
Masons of Golconde yesterday sent to New Liberty a large
quantity of breadstuffs, potatoes, etc. At Alida Point this
morning at 7:30, a Government light was seen in a tree ten feet
above the water and still burning. It had lodged there during
the gale.

At May's Landing, Ky., opposite Golconda, a two story
house and a warehouse were swept away; the chimneys are
standing. At Empire Landing, Ill., the water is up to the
eaves of the warehouse. At Trabue Coal Landing, Ky., one
house was swept away.

CARRSVILLE, KY.

Arrived at 2 p. m., February 23d.—LaMarr's house opposite,
in Illinois, was swept away during the gale. During the storm
Mr Crotser's warehouse was damaged about $500 worth, and
he lost 500 empty barrels While making the landing at Carrsville we struck, with force, the rocks and knocked a hole in the
bow under the guard. Being above the water line it caused
no material delay, and after leaving Carrsville it was caulked
with cotton and wadding.

ROSE CLARE, ILL.

Arrived February 23d. During the storm five houses
were set afloat, but were caught after drifting around town.
The warehouse is a total wreck. I visited Maggie, Katie and
Roland Hogan, who were sick on the down trip, and found them
all recovered. Mrs. Dr. Ledynski is well and gone. L. Rick.
ets was found suffering with chills and fever and medicine was

left for him. Two thousand rations were left for Rose Clar^c and one thousand for Barnett's Landing which is opposite, in Kentucky. The wind was off shore, consequently not much damage was done by the storm.

ELIZABETHTOWN, ILL.

February 23 —On the trip down this place did not require assistance, but since the storm a change has taken place. Seven houses have been washed away and twenty-five families are destitute, and but for the fact that the wind was off shore the destruction would have been much greater. The river has fallen three inches since yesterday. Mr. C. W. Morris, pastor of the M. E. Church, stated that there were many destitute. Several houses are floating in the town but they are tied by ropes. A Relief Committee has been formed consisting of H. B. Renfro, County Clerk, President; S. D. Miller, S. L. Womack, Henry Ferrill, A. H. McFarland, James Hetherington, Treasurer, and Jessie Kirkham, Secretary. Two thousand and six hundred rations were left with the Relief Board for distribution to the destitute.

SEVERE ACCIDENT.

After placing the boat in quarters for the night Captain MacGowan while crossing a plank slipped and fell a distance of twelve feet, striking upon his side and causing a semi-contusion of the chest and a partial dislocation of the lower ribs. He was taken on board by two men, and I reduced the dislocation, bandaged the chest and placed him in a comfortable condition for the night.

We left at 5:45 a. m., February 24th, 1884.—Captain MacGowan is feeling some better this morning, and though it is very painful to him, he is nevertheless up attending to duty.

At Brown's Point, opposite Weston, the gale made great havoc among the trees, hundreds of them being broken down. We made no stop till we reached Caseyville, where we arrived at 9 a. m.

CASEYVILLE, KY.

February 24, 1884.—Great damage has been caused by the storm of last Tuesday at this place. Below the wharf-boat are several acres of floating houses completely demolished. Fifty buildings were washed away by the storm, among them the Methodist Church, Christian Church, Dyer & Winson, largest dry goods house in town; Heine's two buildings, ruined; Smallwind, two houses all gone; Henry Walter, general sewing machine agent, lost a large number of machines; Chas. Rehm, butcher, house and barn; W. E Vaniway, residence. The Postoffice, which was a three story brick building, fell in on Thursday morning and is a complete wreck. Four boys were sleeping in it but they escaped unhurt. Postmaster Brooks stated that he lost a large amount of stamps, envelopes, postal cards, etc. The books were saved. E. K Eberly & Co's large hardware house is gone. Dr. Barkley's house is demolished. Henry Heine was injured internally by falling bricks. There is not a safe brick house in the place. Gierson, Ruby & Co's. large tobacco warehouse is a total wreck. The livery stable belonging to John Graham is gone and one horse is lost. The waves ran twenty feet high. Seventy-five thousand dollars will hardly cover the loss. There has been no State aid yet. The storm commenced at three in the afternoon and lasted until two in the morning. The hotel of B. C. Wells is ruined. Dyer's Exposition (agricultural building) is destroyed. The Casey ville Enterprise building is greatly damaged and the paper can not be published The building next to it is a wreck. The river is seven inches higher than last year, and the town is full of floating household goods.

John F. Hart has his grocery on a barge covered with a tent. Four thousand extra rations were left for here and De-Koven. The boat took coal at Colonel Sellers' landing. Commu. nicated with the steamer Osceola, eight miles below Shawneetown. She left twenty thousand rations at Shawneetown, and has thirty thousand for Paducah and twenty-five thousand rations for any other needy point. A list of the rations as issued by us was given the Osceola for their guidance.

SHAWNEETOWN, ILL.

February 24th, 1 p. m.' The great storm of Tuesday has been most destructive to the place; but fortunately the direction of the wind prevented the entire destruction of the town, as

must necessarily have followed had the wind been on shore.
The hills in the rear of the town afforded some protection, but
as it was, two hundred houses were washed away by the waves,
and one hundred entirely demolished. Shawneetown is indeed
at present in a most deplorable condition, and the suffering and
destitution is great. Hundreds of families are without homes,
and many without shelter or clothing. Mayor J. W. Millspaugh
has issued an appeal for aid. The storm was most violent and
the waves ran so high and with such force that many boats and
skiffs were completely demolished. Some of the more important places that suffered during the storm are A. K. Lowe's
new stable, washed away: The new school house, made of
brick, and three stories high, has all the windows broken and
the west wall has fallen out. There are only two houses left on
"Nigger Flat." Mike Golden lost two houses, and Mr. Powell
a portion of his house. McMunchy & Barr's large corn crib was
swept away and lodged on the levee. The O. & M. depot has
turned around with the front facing east. John Finnigan's
house has gone to pieces, while two houses, the property of
Mrs. Susan Sellar and John Friers, have turned over on their
sides. Mayor Millspaugh's wife had a very narrow escape from
being drowned during the storm. Left Shawneetown at 1:30
in the afternoon.

At Harris' Landing, below Uniontown, a house and barn
are gone. All gone out of Mississippi Bend where, before the
storm, there were six houses. Poker Point, house gone. Dan
Isham, in Indiana, a point opposite Mississippi Bend, all gone.
Peter Kittle's new house on New Mound is gone. A barn at the
old Ingram place, and a house and barn at Billett Place, all gone.

UNIONTOWN, KY,

Arrived at 3 p. m. Great damage was done here by the
storm. The river has fallen fourteen inches. Many people
are still suffering and five thousand extra rations were left.
Sixty-one houses were destroyed in the storm and the loss is
estimated at about eighty thousand dollars. John Roech's dis-
tillery was damaged to the amount of three thousand dollars;
Gus Franklin lost five thousand dollars worth of dry goods, and
eight thousand dollars worth of tobacco and lumber were swept

away from Williams' tobacco factory. Almost every stable in town has been carried away and the people are suffering for fuel. The waves rolled into the town fifteen feet high and demolished nearly everything they struck.

Savage's Landing, Ky., two houses and one barn are gone.

Gasper's Landing, two large barns and a house are gone.

Henry C. Dixon's two two-story houses are gone.

MT. VERNON, IND.

Arrived at 5 p. m. Three thousand extra rations were left, except in meat, which, being short, was made up in other articles. This completes our supply.

The gallant little steamer Carrie Caldwell, has made the extraordinary average time of seven miles per hour against the terrific current now in the Ohio. The run of fifteen miles, from Uniontown to Mt. Vernon, was made in one hour and forty-two minutes. We remained at Mt. Vernon all night and left at 5:45 the following morning for West Franklin where we arrived at 8:45 in the morning.

WEST FRANKLIN.

February 25th, 1884—Several houses were washed away during the storm. A warehouse and a church were ruined. There is drift of all kinds in the town. We only stopped a few minutes at West Franklin when we resumed our trip up the river and arrived at Evansville, at 10 a. m., February 25, 1884. Captain McGowan at once discharged the boat and returned to his station at Louisville, Ky.

The following summary will show the entire cost of the trip and the distribution of the rations.

Number of rations purchased at Evansville	. . . . .	75,000
" " " Paducah	. . . . . .	10,000
Total	. . . .	85,000
Cost of rations purchased at Evansville	. . . . .	$9,594 92
" " " Paducah	. . . . . .	1,440 50
Total	. . . .	$11,035 42
Cost of boat for ten days @ $125 per day	. . . .	1,250 00
Total cost of trip	. . . .	$12,285 42

7

The average cost per ration purchased at Evansville was 12¾c.
The average cost per ration purchased at Paducah   was 14½c.
The average cost per ration as distributed, including the
     cost of transportation, was 12¼c

The whole number of rations issued from the steamer
Carrie Caldwell between Evansville, Indiana, and Cairo, Illinois,
from February 16th to February 25, inclusive, were as follows:

West Franklin... 1,000
Mt. Vernon... 8,500
Uniontown.. 15,000
Raleigh 1,000
Shawneetown 15,000
Caseyville, DeKoven, Cooper's Mines 5,000
Cave-in-Rock 1,000
Elizabethtown 2,600
Rose Clare.. 4,000
Barnett's Landing 1,000
Carrsville... 1,000
Golconda 10,000
Smithland 4,000
New Liberty.. 6,000
Paducah.. 10,000
Brooklyn and Stringtown 5,000
Metropolis... 5,000
Joppa 500
Bird's Point and Wickliff 5,000
                                                                      ——————
     Total 100,600

It will be observed that the whole number of rations purchased were 85,000 and the whole number distributed were
100,600. This difference is accounted for from the fact the
rations were purchased in bulk and distributed by weight, the
regular army ration being the standard. One hundred thousand
and 600 rations were therefore distributed at a cost to the Government of $12,285 42, or 12¼ cts per ration. These rations
were calculated to supply ten thousand people with food for ten
days.

SECOND TRIP

OF THE

United States Relief Boat Carrie Caldwell,

TO AID THE

Ohio River Flood Sufferers:

Evansville, Indiana, to Wickliff, Kentucky

AND RETURN,

March 3d to March 14th, 1884, inclusive.

Captain A. B. MacGowan, 12th U. S. Infantry, Commanding

It was only a few days after the return of the steamer
Carrie Caldwell from her first relief expedition down the river
that information was received in this city, and later at Washington, D. C, to the effect that the suffering was still great
throughout the bottom lands and that more assistance would be
required between here and Cairo by the sufferers from the Ohio
River flood. The water had fallen many feet in the mean time,
some farmers had moved back into their wet and dilapidated
houses, many had left their high places of safety and returned
to their farms only to find their houses destroyed and no shelter
except what temporary coverings they might erect; and many
others were still remaining where they had been driven by the
recent flood, when to add to the misery and suffering already
existing it turned extremely cold. Then was the time above
all others when energetic measures were needed for the speedy
relief of the thousands of people without homes or shelter other
than tents or rudely constructed sheds, whose supply of food
and fuel was limited, and their clothing meagre in the extreme.
Honorable Robert T. Lincoln, Secretary of War, was at once

apprised of the situation of affairs and he lost no time in again detailing Captain A. B. MacGowan, through Assistant Quartermaster General Rufus Saxton, at Louisville, Ky., to proceed to Evansville, Indiana, purchase 100,000 rations, with bedding and comforts, and start to the relief of the suffering people between Evansville, Ind., and Cairo, Ill. Accordingly Capt. MacGowan left Louisville, accompanied by his wife, on March 2d, and arrived in Evansville the following morning, Monday, March 3d. Here he was joined by Mr. George W. Cowlam and son, also from Louisville. Mr. Cowlam, who is the Indiana State Agent of the U. S. Life Insurance Company, was detailed by Assistant Quartermaster General Rufus Saxton, as chief clerk to Captain A. B. MacGowan to assist him in the relief transactions during the trip. As soon as Captain MacGowan arrived the Carrie Caldwell was again chartered and the contracts for furnishing the supplies awarded to the following parties, who were the lowest bidders:

William Caldwell.

1000 pounds	yeast powder @ 9½c	. . . . . .	$	95 00
8000 "	Arbuckle roasted Coffee 17⅞c			1,430 00
2100 "	soap @ 4c	. . . . .		84 00
14867 "	sugar @ 6¾c	. . . . .		1,003 52
780 bushels	Irish potatoes @ 45c ⅌ bushel	.		351 00
91 "	onions, @ 80c ⅌ bushel	. . .		72 80

Amount $3,036 32

Mackey, Nisbet & Co.

1696 pairs blankets @ $2 50 . . . . $42 40
2004 comforts @ $1 25 . . . . 25 05

Amount $67 45

W. M. Akin and Son.

75,000 pounds salt sides (bacon) 1541 pieces, @9¾c $7,312 50

Elles & Knauss

100 barrels flour @ $5 25 . . . . $525 00
180 " " 5 00 . . . . 900 00

Amount . . . . ♦ $1,425 00

George P. Heilman.

625 sacks corn meal @ $1 10	$687 50
50 barrels hominy grits @ $2 90	145 00

Amount $832 50

It is proper to state in this connection that a generosity was manifested by the Evansville merchants of whom the supplies were purchased, both for this trip and the preceding one, and for them to place their items at the lowest possible figures commensurate with the emergency. The large amount of groceries purchased from William Caldwell hardly made an impression upon his large wholesale and retail house on First Street ; while the firm of W. M. Akin & Son could easily have furnished double the amount of bacon supplied if required. The blankets and comforts came from the large wholesale house of Mackey, Nisbet & Co., on First Street, the largest house of the kind in the Southwest. They were delivered on the boat in two hours from the time the order was given. Owing to the severity of the weather and the long continued exposure to which the sufferers had been subjected, sickness was very prevalent among the refugees and many deaths had occurred. Seeing the importance of medical aid to those who were beyond the reach of local physicians, I was again detailed by Surgeon General John B. Hamilton of the U. S. Marine Hospital Service, to accompany the expedition in charge of the Medical Department and to administer to the sufferers wherever found. Under these instructions I at once telegraphed the Secretary of War for authority to purchase a complete outfit of medicines and disinfectants for distribution upon the trip, and received in reply cart blanche directions to purchase what articles were necessary and the Department would attend to the bill. This was very graceful on the part of Honorable Robert T. Lincoln, and I at once began receiving bids for furnishing the necessary medical supplies. The St. George Drug Store, under the management of Mr. C. G. Harris, Ph. G., being the lowest bidder, received the contract, the bill for the same amounting to $112 92. Principal among the items was a large quantity of disinfectants for use in cleansing the houses which had been submerged thus rendering them hygienically habitable.

All Monday night and Tuesday, March 3d and 4th the employes were busy loading the boat, and early Wednesday morning we departed on our trip down the river, The summary of the 100,000 rations is as follows:

625 sacks corn meal,	14,867 lbs sugar,
50 barrels hominy grits,	2,100 lbs soap,
280 barrels flour,	780 bushels potatoes,
75,000 lbs bacon,	91 bushels onions,
1,000 lbs yeast powders,	1,696 pairs blankets,
8,000 lbs coffee,	2,004 comforts (bed),

In addition to these were the medicines and disinfectants The total cost of the outfit amounting to $19,464 24.

The following is the revised log of the second trip of the Carrie Caldwell as kept by me at the time.

STEAMER CARRIE CALDWELL,
March 5th, 1884.

It being too late to make a departure Tuesday evening we remained at the wharf-boat and left Evansville at 6:25 a. m. Wednesday morning, March 5th.

The following are the officers of the boat:

Capt A. B. MacGowan, 12th U. S. Infantry, commanding.

Dr. R. P. M. Ames, Assistant Surgeon U. S. Marine Hospital Service, in charge of the Medical Department.

Mr. George W. Cowlam, Chief Clerk.

John Weed, Captain of steamer Carrie Caldwell.

J. F. Crane, Mate   "   "   "

Henry Matheney, Pilot   "   "   "

Eugene Brady, 1st Clerk,   "   "   "

George Swearanger, 2d Clerk "   "   "

John Orr, Engineer   "   "   "

Edward Lamb, Steward   "   "   "

Captain MacGowan was accompanied by his wife and Mrs. R. P. M. Ames was also a mmember of the party. Mr. Cowlam was assisted by his son George S. Cowlam. Rev. Dr. E. T. Howe also accompanied the boat. He is the pastor of the First Congregational Church, Peoria, Ill., and Chairman of the Relief Committee of Peoria. His mission is to make a personal investigation of all suffering, and then report to the Relief Committee, when the funds will be sent to the places needing it. They have already placed at the disposal of the Red Cross Society a large sum of money, clothing, etc., and Mr. Howe has now $2,000 on which to draw. He will confine his attention to the Illinois shore, and in all probability not go farther than Shawneetown.

WEST FRANKLIN, IND.

Arrived at 8:45 a. m.—Met Mr. Geo. W. Lutz, Postmaster, who stated that the place is now in comfortable circumstances. A large number of fences were washed away, but will soon be rebuilt.

Only fifty-three people were in want of help and rations for this number were left. A large quantity of disinfectants were left, and the following sick people were visited by myself and medicines and directions left : May J. Williams, pneumonia; Abner Lockhart, pneumonia ; Francis and Barbara Gussman, chills and fever ; Mary Dugan, dysentery ; Lucy Hogan, double pneumonia. In addition 50 lbs of copperas and 30lbs of flax seed meal were left.

ALZEY POINT, KY.

Arrived at 10 a. m.—Everything is gone at this point. The only house in the neighborhood is 'Squire Long's, which is one half a mile above, a two story house, and one small one back in the woods one mile distant. We stopped fifteen min. utes, and whistling aid for that length of time, no one being in sight, we left. The river is three feet below the level of the bank. A few household utensils were seen lying around, but the destruction and desolation as far as the eye could reach is the state of affairs.

No stop at Crutchfield's Landing as not a house is left.

At Pritchett's Landing, one-half mile below Alzey, we met Mr. James Pritchett, who stated that there were thirty people suffering there. back of Alzey twelve more, but there was no place to leave supplies, and therefore, at their request, we left them at Mt. Vernon. Ed Stiles was found sick at Pritchett's Landing with congestive fever, and medicines were left. Supplies for these two places were left with C. P. Kline, Mt. Vernon.

MT. VERNON, IND.

Arrived at 11 a. m., March 5, 1884 —Captain MacGowan
and myself met the Relief Committee, consisting of Mayor
Smith, Major Milner, Treasurer; Col. Owen, Secretary and
others Mr. Milner says they have sixty-five families entirely
destitute, not a thing left for them except the clothes they have
on. These families average five each and are from the bottoms
as far down as Point Township to the Wabash on the Indiana
shore. There are forty-eight families of six in a family from
the Kentucky bottoms, opposite. These are totally helpless,
having not a thing left. The Relief Committee state that they
have supplies enough left to last ten days. Captain MacGowan
therefore, left rations to last to the end of the month for 805
people, rations for fifteen days, amounting to 12,075 rations in
all, for Mt. Vernon, Point township, Walnut Bend, Crutchfield's
and Pritchett's, also Alzey. If tents could be provided many
of the people could help themselves by the end of the month.
Of 132 houses in Walnut Bend fifty-three are gone, leaving the
families with nothing. At Point Township fifty-one families
are homeless and destitute. In the aggregate there are here
six hundred and fourteen people, representing one hundred
and thirteen families, entirely destitute, without even a sack or
a blanket; one hundred and ninety two people with nothing but
a bed or bureau, or an extra coat. A great many are sick;
fifty-three adults and sixty-eight children. Pneumonia, chills
and fever and dysentery are the chief complaints I left with
the Relief Committee a full amount of medicines and a large
quantity of disinfectants, such as carbolic acid, etc. In addition
to the rations 207 pairs of blankets and 200 quilts are left. Rev.
E. T. Howe ascertained that a liberal donation of lumber for
building purposes would be very acceptable for use in the lower
Wabash bottoms. Mr. Howe will report this to the Peoria
Relief Committee, and the lumber will be bought and shipped
by rail. Mr. Howe left with the Mt. Vernon Relief Committee
one basket of clothing containing twelve good suits. Mt.
Vernon has received, with the present donation, 28,575 rations
from the Government of the United States. Left Mt. Vernon
at 2 p. m.

UNIONTOWN, KY,

Arrived at 3:15 p. m. The town does indeed present a desolate appearance, not a street but what is full of demolished houses, barns, massive trees, and all kinds of drift. A large house, broken in two, lies in front of the Grand Hotel. Lower Second Street for one-half a mile is impassable, while the whole upper part of the town is one complete wreck—destruction as far as the eye can reach. The river is down now in its banks, unveiling the terrible destruction left in its track. Some effort will be made in a few days to start to clean up the town. All summer will not see it done. The entire loss is estimated at from $150,000 to $175,000. There are fifty houses flat on Upper Third Street, and not one fifth of the owners can afford to rebuild. The State aid, in funds, is now being used in repairing, which is very slow as workmen can not be had, from the fact that all those needing work, mostly negroes, are getting all they want to eat and wont do a thing. Everything is peaceful, however. Families from farms five miles below are in town for help Their houses, barns, etc., are all gone, and unless they can have temporary shelter they never will be able to cultivate their farms or again erect houses People also come from the bot toms above town and from the Indiana shore. The Relief Committee stated that they had all the food that they could use for their own town people, but would need a little for those that have come in upon them. The town Marshal, Mr. Crane, estimates thirty families completely destitute of even bed clothing in town, and about one hundred families that have come in from above and below, needing clothing. Left 100 pairs of blankets and 150 quilts. Rations for the end of the month, 3,125 in all. Left Uniontown at 5 p. m. and dropped two miles below where we remained all night.

March 6th, 1884.—Resumed our trip at 6 a. m. for points below on the river. No accident, every one happy, all well.

SHAWNEETOWN, ILL,

Arrived at 7:15 a. m. The town does not present the amount of destruction that a person might suppose from reports and previous condition. Repairing is beginning, and soon business will be resumed and everything go on as before th

8

flood. Mayor Millspaugh states that there are now about 800 people destitute, and 200 without anything to sleep on or cover themselves but their one suit. He thinks by the end of the month all will be cared for and the suffering at an end. This district is thirty-five miles long on the Illinois shore, from New Haven to Saline below. Kentucky sends over twenty-five families. As soon as the trains are running they will be all right. The rations left were 12,000; blankets, 100; quilts and comforts, 100.

BLACKBURN, KY.,

Opposite Shawneetown. The Postmaster, Mr. Durick, is living on a barge, but his family are back on the hills. Only a few persons are here as yet. The place is ruined. Two boxes of clothing were taken on at Shawneetown and left here, being donated by the Red Cross. Blackburn has been receiving rations from Shawneetown, but a full supply has now been left for 100 people. Twelve families (60 people) are destitute. The territory for four miles above Blackburn and seven miles below, receives aid from here. There are ten families without clothing—100 blankets were left. Mr. Durick received $25 cash some time ago from the St. Louis branch of the Red Cross to purchase medicines for the sick. Eight sick people were found—Burnett 3, Goodman 2, Hamilton 3. Pneumonia and chills were the principal diseases. A full supply of medicines were left, and also disinfectants.

CASEYVILLE, KY.

Arrived at 11:30 a. m. Left at 1:30 p. m. The steamer Oil City is lying a wreck at the wharf-boat. The town is in a deplorable condition, all the streets being impassable from the large number of houses that are demolished and are lying around the town. Mr. Brooks, Postmaster, states that the work of repairing will begin as soon as possible. The total damage is estimated at $75,000. Four boxes of clothing were left here yesterday by order of the Red Cross Association for distribution by the Relief Committee. There are fifty-two demolished houses in the town, and nine-tenths of the owners can never rebuild. While walking through the town Mr. W. A. Delancy was seen riding on horseback carrying a coffin to bury his child that died yesterday of pneumonia, four miles below the town. Pneumonia and chills are very prevalent, and many deaths are expected. Three thousand rations and fifty blankets were left. We then left and went to Shotwell's Mines, above the town, for coal. Above Caseyville the two-story frame house that was washed away from Mackey's plantation at Pacific Point was seen lodged on the old Crabtree Place in Shawneetown Bend, fifteen miles below its proper site.

At the Shotwell Mines Landing we met Dr. P. G. Kelsey, who very kindly offered to transport our party to the mines and give us a thorough inspection of the coal fields. While the boat was coaling Mrs. Dr. R. P. M. Ames, Mrs. Captain MacGowan, Capt. Weed, Clerk Brady, myself and several others took the engine "Arthur Kelsey" and several empty coal cars of fifty bushels capacity each, with Dr. P. G. Kelsey, and ran down to the mines 1½ miles distant. The party then took cars and entered the Moorehead slope and descended to the bottom of the slope a distance of 2000 feet, taking ten minutes to make the descent. Once in the mine we found a perfect village. The avenues and roads extend in every direction for miles. Each entrance has an air passage parallel with it, and the ventilation of the mine is perfect in the remotest corner. At the foot of the slope, and 200 feet under ground, is a large pump, which keeps the mines perfectly dry. There are eight to ten veins of coal from 4 to 4-8 feet thick, and all these are worked. The capacity of the mine is 10,000 bushels a day. At present only one hundred miners are employed. Dr. J. H. Ames is the mine physician. There are two large veins, forty feet apart, from which nearly all the coal is taken. These veins are reached by avenues with a slope of one foot to twelve feet. The party were greatly indebted to Superintendent Whitehead, who conducted the party through the mines with Dr. P. G Kelsey. Dr. P. G. Kelsey is a prominent owner and stockholder, and is giving great credit in his management of the mines. The miners receive three cents per bushel of coal, and average $3 per day, or 100 bushels. Heavy rain and great fog prevented our departure for points below, and we remained at Shotwell's all night.

Friday, March 7, 1884. Left Shotwell's at 5:45 a. m. During the night we parted with the Rev. Mr. Howe, of Peoria, he taking the steamer Hopkins for Evansville on his way home. Mr. Howe has given the sufferers all his personal attention and has been untiring in his efforts to ferret out all the distress. Much aid can now be better and more substantially given by the Peoria Relief Committee, as they will be guided by his personal experience. Several boxes of clothing were left by him for distribution below.

WESTON, KY.

Arrived at 6:30 a. m. Thomas Lamb, Chairman of the Trustees of the town, states that at Lamb's coal mines and at Bell's coal mines there are, with the destitute in the town, about fifty-one people needing aid. Four thousand rations were left, and 124 blankets and 24 quilts. The town comprises 300 people. The water has fallen 25 feet. Considerable sickness prevails.

FORD'S FERRY, KY.

Arrived at 7:45 a, m. Mr. E. E. Jennings, Postmaster, states there are but three families that were drowned out. They all have plenty to eat, are not destitute, and practically require nothing. After mature consideration, however, Mr. Jennings thought that Mr. John Summer's family of five might require help and 100 rations were issued. Mrs. Paris was found sick with pneumonia and medicines were left. Mr. Jennings further stated that he himself would require aid, and he thought it right that we should leave money for him to build his house and barn. He had been told that the Government would make all repairs necessary or required, and he proposed to see that he had his share and that Government clerks did not pocket the funds. The misunderstanding was explained and he was satisfied with hog and hominy.

CAVE-IN-ROCK, ILL.

Arrived at 8:30 a. m. Mr. J. J. Goodwin, Postmaster, states they are in comparatively comfortable circumstances, but a little food would be acceptable; 2,000 rations were therefore left. There were several families that were needing clothing, and several suits were left. Anderson, with six in family, was suppled; also the widow Belk. There is a great amount of sickness and the local physician has his hands full. I saw fifteen and left them a full supply of medicines that would last them fifteen days, besides a large supply of disinfectants.

HURRICANE, KY.

Arrived at 9:45 a. m. Joseph Guess, the "boss" of the town, could not be found, but some parties on shore stated that there were only two families that were wanting anything, and they would take $50 apiece instead of provisions. Of course the $50 was not left, but a check well be made out for the amount and furnished them direct from Paducah—next year. No supplies were left. Just before reaching Hurricane we blew the whistle off and are now without one. Quite an excitement prevailed for the time being, among the ladies, as the pilot-house was filled with steam. The accident, however, did no damage other than the ruin of the whistle.

ELIZABETHTOWN, ILL.

Arrived at 10:20 a. m. We met the Relief Committee, J. H. Renfrau, President Town Board; J. V. Vineyard, Secretary They stated there were twelve families absolutely destitute, and that these were from the bottom three miles above and one mile below, and from the Kentucky shore opposite; 2,000 rations were left, ten blankets and two comforts, for distribution by the Town Marshal, C. L. Womack.

ROSE CLARE, ILL.

Arrrived March 7, at 12 noon. Mr. Fields, who had received our supplies before, came aboard as soon as the boat touched the shore, and stated that the people felt under obligations to the Government for the assistance rendered them, and that any remarks passed before were not called for, and were made by some persons not sane at the time. Mr. Fields further stated that Charles Kilgron made the remarks passed before, and the people were very sorry for it. They were very grateful for all the supplies left to-day. Several suits of clothing were left for parties in Rose Clare, and some for those in the bottoms in Ken-tucky, opposite. A large number of persons were sick. I Saw at least 100 sick people. Among them were the following bad cases. John Hogan, chills and fever; Eliza Martin, dysentery; Mrs. Harrison Tyron and child, dysentery; Mrs. Gibson, pneumonia; James Laden, congestion of the liver; Mrs. James Laden, pneumonia; and John Laden, compound fracture of the forearm. The latter occurred from a fall yesterday and was dressed by me to-day. The suffering of the young man was terrible before the dressing. Medicines were left for all and a full supply of disinfectants. Clothing was also left with Mr. Frank Sullins for himself, wife and three children. Timothy Patterson was treated for rheumatism. Four thousand rations were left, five pairs of blankets and two quilts.

CARRSVILLE, KY.

Arrived at 1:30 p. m. Raining hard and freezing. Robert Crotser says he had great trouble in distributing the supplies left at this place on our former trip, owing to the dissatisfaction of the people, etc., and don't care to do it this time. The town is not suffering much, but some people from above and below come in for aid. Mr. Bridges says that there are eight families with fifty persons above needing aid and thirty-five persons below, at Breeden's Landing. None are destitute of bedding except Mr. Hardin's family, who were burnt out and are now sleeping on straw. Hazel Webb and family of six were visited and all found sick with measles. They were attended to by me and medicines left. The following were left with Mr. Vick for distribution: Rations, 2,000; 20 blankets; 2 quilts.

GOLCONDA, ILL.

Arrived at 3 p. m. The Relief Committee state that they do not require any assistance. In fact, the supplies we left them on the last trip held out till day before yesterday, when they sold the remaining articles and deposited the amount received, $193, in the bank as a relief fund. John Glass' house, in the bottoms, was destroyed during the late gale, by fire, the wind blowing open the door and upsetting the stove. Mr. Glass lost all he possessed. As long as the supplies were issued free the negroes could not be hired to work for even $10 a day. It is very stormy and we will remain all night; 4:45 p. m. and foggy.

Saturday March 8th, 1884. A real pleasant evening was spent at Golconda yesterday. The representatives of Golconda could not do too much to show their appreciation of the assistance rendered them during the flood by the U. S. Government, and kept open house and extended arms during our stay. Early in the evening a large party of ladies and gentlemen, headed by the Golconda Cornet Silver Band of sixteen pieces, led by Professor Swan, of New York, came on the boat and took full possession. We were treated to several excellent concert pieces and three opera selections. Too much praise cannot be given the band for the perfect rendition of their selections, and Golconda may well be proud of such an efficient association of musicians. At 9 o'clock, after a grand march, dancing commenced and lasted till 12, when the party took their departure, but not as silently as they came.

The affair was a most enjoyable one, and one that will long be remembered. Unfortunately the night was not of the best, as a drizzling rain set in early. The ladies, nothing daunted, bravely bid defiance to the rain and came in force. Among the ladies present were; Misses Ruth and Flora Steyer, daughters of Mayor Theodore Steyer, Misses Carrie Pierce and Mary Pierce, daughters of Major A. T. Pearce, Miss Mamie Young, Daughter of Dr. Young; Mrs. Matt Williams, daughter of Mayor Steyer, Mrs. Dr. Young, Mrs. Dr. R. P. M. Ames and Mrs. A. B. MacGowan.

Gentlemen—Mayor Theodore Steyer, Judge Thomas, Major A. T. Pearce, Dr. Young, Captain Arthur Cole, T. M. McCoy, Thos. MacGowan, Abraham Reezer, Philip Field, Captain MacGowan, Mr. Cowlam, myself and many others. The ladies all came to have a good time and enjoy themselves, consequently white kids and low corsage were at a discount. We were only too sorry when the time came for their departure. Major Pierce was acknowledged by all to be the most graceful dancer on the floor. The Major tips them at 250 pounds. After a good sleep we left Golconda at 6 a. m.

COFFEE LANDING, KY.

Arrived at 6:30 a. m. There is one house here in which lives H. B. Walls, wife and four children, all destitute, and two children sick; 1,000 rations were left, 50 blankets and 25 quilts. May and Hattie Walls both sick with pneumonia. They were visited by me and medicines left.

BAY CITY, ILL.

Arrived at 8 a. m.   The high water at this place did not reach the top of the high banks upon which Bay City is placed The warehouse of H. C. Henson was slightly damaged by floating drift.   The Postmaster said they needed no assistance and nothing was left.

BAYOU MILLS, KY.

Arrived at 8:30 a. m.   One thousand rations were left and 12 blankets and 12 quilts.   Some destitution.   Three persons were found sick and medicine left; also disinfectants.

BIRDSVILLE, KY.

Arrived at 9 a. m.   Mr. R. M. Wilson states that there are almost thirty families destitute in and around Birdsville—1,200 rations were left, 12 blankets, 12 quilts, a large quantity of clothing, copperas and flax seed meal.   John Higgins was found sick with congestion of the brain.   He is in a very critical condition.

SMITHLAND, KY.

Arrived at 10:30 a. m.   No provisions are needed, but 100 blankets and 25 quilts were left.   The Relief Committee have done active work   All supplies were left with Mr. W. F. Grayot, of the Relief Committee.

NEW LIBERTY, ILL.

Saturday, March 8.—Arrived at 11:30 a. m.   There are about thirty families destitute at the present time, of food and clothing, in Unionville, below New Liberty, and Hambletsburg, about 720 people in all; 1,000 rations were left, 100 blankets and 50 quilts.   A large quantity of disinfectants were also left in charge of J. A. Simpson, I was asked to investigate the situation of the town as to its needs for money, by a representative of a New York Benefit Club, I found that $250 could be very judiciously expended in repairing houses, and authorized Mr. J. A. Shearer to draw for the amount etc., through Mayor Millspaugh, of Shawneetown, Illinois.

PADUCAH, KY.

Arrived at 1:40 p. m. We met the Relief Committee, represented by Mayor Reed, Major Ashcraft, Rev. Mr. Rogers, of the Episcopal Church, and Judge Campbell. They stated that they had all the food they needed. Rations were being issued twice a week by order of the Mayor from the headquarters in the Old Commercial Bank. The Relief Committee further stated that many people were destitute of clothing and bedding. Consequently 200 blankets were issued and 100 quilts, also all the reserve clothing in the boat. We left Paducah at 3 p. m. Great credit is due Mayor Reed for his care and personal supervision of the distribution of supplies to the flood sufferers.

BROOKLYN, ILL.

Arrived at 2:20 p. m.—Mr. H. D. Hall, who was exposed during the storm, died from the effects of the exposure Tuesday morning. A large supply of medicines were left with Dr. Young. Rations for 600 people, or 6,000 rations were left, 24 blankets and 12 quilts were also left. Left at 4:20 p.m.

METROPOLIS, ILL.

Arrived at 5:15 p. m. I called upon the Mayor, Dr. Norris, and other members of the Relief Committee, and ascertained that they were in a deplorable condition—even worse than at any time during the storm. Four hundred and fifty-one families were relieved out of the last rations left by us, and 5,000 were left by the Osceola. There are thirty families between here and Brooklyn, Ill., colored, that require more assistance than any in town. Rations have to be issued here for a distance of fourteen miles, above and below and back of the place, with 200 people across the river, about 3,000 people in all. All the mills and factories are frozen up or washed away, and there is no employment for the populace. There is more need for relief to-day than at any time since the storm. They have received in all about $800 from outside parties. Their rations lasted till last Monday. Mr. T. S. Stone, of the City Council, states that

!)

there are about seventy families entirely destitute of bedding and clothing. This state of affairs being understood, Captain MacGowan telegraphed General Saxton for 30,000 more rations for Metropolis. We will leave 10,000 here from our supply and await further orders from General Saxton, of Louisville. 340 blankets were left and 200 quilts. We will remain here all night. We now have, after supplying Metropolis, 30,000 rations left for points below,

STEAMER CARRIE CALDWELL, }
Sunday, March 9th, 1884. }

On account of the hour at which we arrived in Metropolis. the large supply of rations were not put ashore until this morning, making it 8 a. m. when we left.

JOPPA, ILL.

Arrived at 8:35 a. m. There is considerable destitution and sickness at this place. One thousand rations were left with D. W. Thompson, Postmaster; also four blankets and one comfort. A large box of clothing was also left and a full supply of quinine and copperas. No supplies have been left here since our last trip. The rain, sleet and cold weather have kept the men from doing any work.

OGDEN'S LANDING, KY.

Arrived at 9:45 a. m. No supplies left.
Arrived at Grand Chain, Ill., at 10:15 a. m. Thomas Bartleson states that no supplies are needed.

UPPER CALEDONIA, ILL.

Arrived at 11 a. m. Thirty people are destitute and 1,000 rations were left, also 20 blankets and 2 quilts—all in charge of John Mohr. Henry Anderson was found sick with pneumonia, and medicines were left also for Berry Hamilton, who was sick. My last supply of disinfectants were left here. If we go below Cairo more medicines must be purchased. Supplies were also left at Upper Caledonia for Turner's Landing.

TERRELL'S LANDING, KY.,

Passed at 11:50 a. m. The place is all washed away. No stop. A landing was made though on the Illinois shore at a place called Cook's Landing, just opposite Terrell's, where we arrived at 12 (noon). I met W. S. Rogers and ascertained that several parties were sick. The patients being a long way back in the hills I did not visit them, but left a full supply of medicine for them with W. S. Rogers. Six hundred rations, 30 blankets and 12 quilts were also left.

MOUND CITY.

Arrived at 1:15 p. m. Six thousand rations, 180 blankets and 120 quilts were left in charge of Mr. Hogan to be distributed throughout the bottom lands back of Mound City and back of the Kentucky shore opposite.

CAIRO, ILL.

Arrived at 2:50 p. m. Past assistant Surgeon John A. Benson, of the U. S. Marine Hospital Service, was at once seen, and stated that he had personally superintended the distribution of the last supplies, and that the following was needed in the vicinity of Cairo: At Wickliff, Ky., there were twenty-five families without clothing; at Bird's Point, Mo., twenty-five families; Reelfoot Landing, five families; Norfolk, Mo., four families; Dog Tooth Bend, ten families, and in the bottom lands between here and Beech Ridge, Ill., thirty families. About 100 families in all. Six thousand rations were therefore left at Cairo in charge of past assistant Surgeon Benson; also 600 blankets and 400 quilts, to be distributed at the above places.

During the evening Dr. and Mrs. R. P. M. Ames were entertained right socially at the Halliday by the Cairo Relief Committee. Dr. Benson desires to express his thanks for the kindness on the part of Mr. R. W. Miller, who freely tendered the use of his warehouse for the storage of the supplies, and personally superintending the sacking of the flour—supplying the sacks himself.

We arrived in Cairo all right and awaited telegraphic orders.

March 10, Monday, at 6 a. m., J. C. Pressnel and John L. Vick, of Smithland, Ky., came aboard and stated that a great mistake had been made on the part of the Relief Committee in refusing rations when in need there. They stated Mr. Grayot, of Smithland, who had received the quilts and blankets, did not know the wants of the town, and by the advice and direction of the Relief Committee these gentlemen were sent to tell us the state of affairs and have some rations left on our return at Smithland. They stated there were between seventy-five and one hundred families perfectly destitute of food, clothing and bedding. Captain MacGowan looked into the matter, and will leave them all we have left on our return trip. We also crossed the Mississippi to Bird's Point, Mo., leaving Cairo at 7 a. m. and arriving at Bird's Point at 8 a. m. Great difficulty was experienced in crossing on account of the floating ice which was coming down the Mississippi in large fields. We found from Mr. Thompson Bird that twenty-five families were destitute, and 1,000 rations were left for this place and Norfolk; also 24 blankets and 12 quilts. These were to go fifteen miles back in the bottoms. I found the following sick here: Wiley Maughun, with pneumonia; J. M. Johnson, Sarah Johnson and Martha Johnson, chills and fever; C. J. Johnson, pneumonia; Patrick Barker, dysentery; Anthony Bird, erysipelas. One of the Johnson family died this morning of heart disease, and I was called in to pronounce it death or suspended animation. Death was the decision. We left Bird's Point at 8:45 a. m. and went down the Mississippi to Wickliff, Ky., where we arrived at 9:15. We met the Relief Committee, consisting of John Walen, J. F. Cocker and Thomas Elliott. They came out to us in skiffs, down Willow Creek, and stated that supplies for fifty people were all they needed for themselves, and at Jefferson, just below; 1,000 rations were left, 40 blankets and 24 quilts. We then turned back to Cairo, which we left at 1 p. m., on our

RETURN TRIP.

March 10. Captain MacGowan has been instructed that the steamer City of Frankfort will send by the Evansville and Cairo packet, the following to Metropolis in answer to his telegram of the 8th inst: Four thousand rations, 25 tents, 450 quilts and 500 blankets. These will be sent from Evansville. We have retained 8,000 rations for Smithland, which will, when delivered, complete our list of supplies. Captain MacGowan wishes to express his thanks for the aid and valuable assistance rendered him in assigning supplies by Mayor Reed of Paducah. Mayor Charles Reed is a typical gentleman of the first water and never allows any of his friends to be forgotten.

A SAD CASE OF DESTITUTION.

As we were steaming off the Kentucky shore we were
hailed about three miles below Turner's Landing at 3:15 p. m.
On going ashore I found a sad state of affairs. Enoch Kenyar
and wife were living on the sand in a tent, while John Holmer
and wife were in a small fishboat—four in all. They had not a
thing to eat except a little meal, which they had been living on
for one week. They stated that they had come down from the
hills, yesterday, with the hope of hailing a boat and getting
something to eat. Mr. Holmer was found quite sick with dysentery. Three hundred rations were left, twelve quilts and
twenty blankets; also a full supply of medicines. We tied up
for the night at Cany Cow Landing, where we arrived at 5:45
in the evening.

March 11.—Left Cany Cow Landing at 6 a. m. Passed
Metropolis at 7:45; no stop. Arrived at Paducah at 10:30.
Will stop only a few minutes and go on to Smithland.

PADUCAH, KY.

March 11, arrived at 10:30 a. m. Mayor Charles Reed stated
that they were now about to close out the supply of rations.
They have been feeding nearly 5,000 people for the past three
weeks, but now all the factories are starting up and all will soon
find work. A few more blankets and quilts were needed for
the few remaining families, and consequently 100 blankets and
200 quilts are left. We were entertained very nicely by the
Mayor, at the Richmond House, and I wish to extend to him
the hearty thanks of Captain MacGowan and myself for his
very kind personal attention to our wants. As before stated,
Mayor Reed is a typical gentleman and never does things by
halves. As a souvenir of the flood, he presented Mrs. Ames
and Mrs. MacGowan with a magnificent photograph, framed in
old gold, 25x30, of the high water in Paducah, 1884, besides
several other smaller ones of different parts of the city. At 11
a. m. we left Paducah on our journey up the river.

SMITHLAND, KY.

Arrived at 1:45 p. m.. Six thousand rations were left.
Mr. W. F. Grayott, Postmaster, states that during the storm

he lost the following from the postoffice: 750 two cent envelopes, 125 postal cards, 24 three cent stamps and 300 postmaster's envelopes. Most of the town mail was lost, but none going out. No registers were lost, but all the office blanks and one mail bag. Left Smithland at 2:30 p. m.

We stopped a few minutes at Bay City, but after leaving Smithland no stop of any amount was made until we reached Lover's Leap, where we tied up for the night. Lover's Leap, so called, is a high bluff of 550 feet overlooking the river on the Illinois shore. It is perfectly perpendicular on the river side, and its summit can only be reached from the river by a dangerous and tedious ascent of hand over hand, from tree to tree and rock to rock, or by going around its base a distance of seven miles and coming up from behind by a gradual ascent. Having an hour to spare after landing, before dark, we attempted the direct ascent and made it after half an hour of hard exhaustive and dangerous climbing. Those that reached the top of the bluff first were Captain Weed, Henry Matheney and Clerk George Swearanger. Later Mrs. Ames and myself reached the top, but no others came, having given out in climbing, and turned back. After a grand survey of the country we lost no time in making the descent, and reached the boat just as a most violent thunder storm burst upon us. We remained here all night and left at 5:45 a. m. for up the river.

March 12.—Stopped a few minutes at Golconda for stores.

ELIZABETHTOWN, ILL.

Arrived at 10 a. m. While at Golconda the steamer Dexter brought a letter of complaint from some of the colored people of Elizabethtown, stating that they did not receive the rations left for them, but that they were being distributed among the whites. On arriving there Captain MacGowan made an investigation and found that the complaint was without foundation. Certain negroes who were not damaged by the high water had demanded supplies, which, of course, were refused; hence the complaint. To make sure, however, that no more trouble would occur Mr. Carter Bryant (colored) was placed on the Relief Committee to assist in the distribution of supplies. Two thousand rations and 48 quilts were left, in addition to those which they had already received. Left Elizabethtown at 10:45 a. m.

CAVE-IN-ROCK, ILL.

Arrived at 12:30. Stopped a few minutes for the ladies to explore the cave.

CASEYVILLE, KY.

Arrived at 2:45 p. m. Met Mr. Hatfield and Dr. Barkley. All are now in a comparatively comfortable condition. The High School building under the charge of Mr. Hatfield, is pronounced unsafe. A Red Cross Society has been organized here. Miss Clara Barton, President of the National Association, left $100, and took the order for several boxes of clothing. We left them 4,000 rations in addition to those they have already received and 100 quilts. Left Caseyville at 3:30 for Shotwell's mine to take on coal. After coaling we proceeded again up the river.

SPECIAL NOTE.

While in Cairo, Captain A. B. MacGowan in conversation with Mayor Halliday, was informed that Senator David Davis had placed at his disposal $10,000 for distribution among those Illinois towns on the Ohio River that were in actual need of it, and asked Captain MacGowan's opinion. After a careful discussion of the subject with myself and Mr. George W. Cowlam Captain MacGowan decided that the following towns should receive the help proffered: Metropolis, New Liberty and Brooklyn should receive one-fourth each of the amount offered, and the remaining one-fourth should be divided equally between New Haven, Rose Clare, Unionville and Stringtown. Permit me to state in this connection that our reasons for refusing Shawneetown are simply these: Shawneetown has received aid from every quarter, both in supplies and money, and while we fully appreciate its past situation, we know from personal observation that it has been better cared for than the smaller and less fortunate towns which we have mentioned. This act of Judge Davis is a most commendable one, and is really the aid that these or any other places along the river now require. They all have food and plenty of it, and money is the great agent that will now place them once more to the front.

SHAWNEETOWN, ILL.

Arrived at 5:45 p. m : Stopped five minutes to leave the mail. At 6 p. m. we ran up to Brown's lower island landing and tied up for the night, three miles above Shawneetown.

March 13—Left Brown's Landing at 5 a. m.

RALEIGH, KY.

Arrived at 5.30 a. m.   Left 1,300 rations with instructions that if more were needed to apply at Uniontown.   We left at 5:45 a. m.   Rations were left with John E. Karr, also 12 quilts.

UNIONTOWN, KY.

Arrived at 6:30.   Left 2,600 rations which we saved for them, these being the last on board.   Our supplies are now all distributed.   Left at 7 a. m.

MT. VERNON, IND,

Arrived at 11 a. m.   Only made a stop of a few minutes to put off mail and telegraph.   We then proceeded to Mt. Nebo where we were compelled to tie up for the night.

March 14.—Left Mt. Nebo this morning at 5:30 a. m. We expect to reach Evansville by 10 a. m.

EVANSVILLE, IND.

March 14th, 1884.   We arrived in Evansville at 10:30 in the forenoon completing the second relief trip of the steamer Carrie Caldwell to the relief of the Ohio River flood sufferers in the spring of 1884.   We have been twelve days out and have distributed all the supplies with which we started.   The medicines and disinfectants have been distributed among nearly three hundred patients, according to their wants.   This ends the second trip of the kind by this boat, and in both instances all the supplies were purchased here, showing conclusively that our markets are by far the best and cheapest on the river.   Had it not been so both trips would have been made and the supplies purchased from Louisville.   The needs of the people that have suffered from the overflow are now nearly supplied.   No more food of any kind will be necessary, and by the time the trip of the Red Cross Society is finished clothing will have been abundantly distributed.   The point now is the erection and repairing of the houses, barns and buildings wrecked or destroyed in order that shelter may be given the farmers of the bottom lands till they can raise a crop, and in this way again make a start. To do this money must be contributed and in such a way that it all will reach the parties most in need. It should only be placed in the hands of those people who have seen and know the exact situation and are capable of distributing and with care and discretion. No more relief will be sent out by the Government, as the work now is practically finished.

The trips of the Carrie Caldwell have been very pleasant ones, if such could be imagined. No accidents have occurred, of note, and nothing to mar the pleasintries of the occasion.

PLACES RELIEVED.

WEDSESDAY, March 5. 1884.

	Rations.	Blankets.	Comforts.
Cave Point, Ky . . . . ⎫	. .	50	24
Union Township, Ind . . . . ⎪			
Knight Township, Ind. . . . ⎭	5000	84	100
West Franklin, Ind.	1000	.	. .
Alzey, Ky . . . . ⎫			
Pritchett, Ky . . . . ⎪			
Crutchfield's, Ky . . . . . . ⎬			
Point Township, Ind . . . . . ⎪			
Walnut Bend, Ky . . . . . . ⎪			
Mount Vernon, Ind . . . . . ⎭	8000		
Uniontown, Ky	5700	100	150
Point Township, lower Ind. . . ⎫			
Raleigh. Ky . . . . ⎭	1300	. .	12

THURSDAY, March 6, 1884.

	Rations.	Blankets.	Comforts.
Shawneetown, Ills . . . . . ⎫	12000	100	100
New Haven, Ills . . . . . . ⎬		-	
Mouth of Saline River . . . . ⎭			
Blackbuurn, Ky	2000	50	. .
DeKoven Mines, Ky	3000	50	25
Coons Ridge, Ky . . . . . . ⎫			
Cooper's Mines, Ky . . . . . ⎪			
Davis' Mines, Ky . . . . . . ⎬			
Commercial Point . . . . . . ⎪			
Caseyville, Ky . . . . ⎭	7000	35	100

10)

Places Supplied.	Rations.	Blankets	Comforts.
Weston, Ky			
Lamb's Mines, Ky			
Bell's Mines, Ky	4000	42	24
Ford's Ferry, Ky			
Cedar Point, Ills			
Frazier Point, Ill	100	1	
Cave-in-Rock, Ills			
Hurricane, Ky	2000	3	1
Rose Clare Ills,			
Barnett's Landing, Ky	4000	5	2
Elizabethtown, Ills			
Crittenden. Co. Ky	4000	5	50
Carrsville, Ky			
Breeden's, Ky	2000	10	2
Parkinson's, Ills			
Golconda, Ills			
Perry's Ferry, Ky			
Coffee Landing, Ky	1000	25	25

SATURDAY, March 8, 1884.

Lover's Leap, Ills			
Bay City, Ills			
Bayou Mills, Ky	1000	6	12
Birdsville, Ky	2000	12	12
Smithland, Ky	8000	50	25
Hamletsburg, Ills			
New Liberty, Ills			
Unionville, Ills	1000	50	50
Paducah, Ky		150	300
Brooklyn, Ills			
Stringtown	6000	12	12
Metropolis, Ills	10000	170	200
Massac, Ills			
Metropolis Landing Ky 25 tents	and4000	250	450

SUNDAY, March 9, 1884.

Joppa, Ills.			
Carico	1000	2	1
Ogden's, Ky			
Grand Chain, Ky			
Caledonia, Ills			
Turner's, Ky	1000	10	10
Pace's Landing, Ky	300	10	12
Terrell's, Ky			
Cook's, Ills	600	15	12
Mound City, Ills	6000	90	120

Places Supplied.	Rations.	Blankets.	Comforts.
MONDAY, March 10, 1884.			
Cairo, Ills			
East Cairo, Ky			
Beach Ridge, Ills			
Dog Tooth Bend, Mo			
Reil Foot, Tenn	6000	300	400
Bird's Point, Mo			
Norfolk, Mo			
Wickliff, Ky	1000	12	12
Fort Jefferson, Ky	1000	20	24
Total,	111,000	1696	2017

Thirteen comforts receipted for more than we had; must have counted in some cases 8 bales as 100 comforts instead of 96.

As soon as we arrived at Evansville the boat was discharged and Captain MacGowan and wife and also Mr. Cowlam and son returned to Louisville, Ky.

The aggregate cost of the trip is as follows:
Whole number of rations purchased at Evansvile . .   100,000

Cost of same $19,351 32
Drugs and disinfectants 112 92

Total $19,464 24
Cost of boat @ $125 per day, 12 days 1,500 00

Entire cost of trip $20,964 24
Average cost per ration purchased at Evansville, including blankets and comforts . . . . $19\frac{1}{3}$ cts.
Average cost per ration distributed including cost of transportation . . . . $18\frac{9}{11}$ cts.
Average cost of ration purchased not including blankets and comforts . . . . $12\frac{2}{3}$ cts.

The following table will show the number of rations distributed between Evansville, Indiana, and Wickliffe, Ky., for the aid of the Ohio River flood sufferers during the spring of 1884, the places relieved, and the number of rations received by each town. In this table all the relief furnished these places is shown except the clothing distributed by the Red Cross Society, and donations of money from outside parties.

PLACES.	First Trip of steamer Carrie Caldwell. Rations.	Second Trip of steamer Carrie Caldwell.			Total amount of rations issued by steamer Carrie Caldwell, on both trips.	Amount of rations issued by the steamer Osceola and by packets from Louisville.	Pairs of Blankets issued by steamer Osceola or packed.	Comforts issued by steamer Osceola or packets.	Total amount of rations issued by the Gov't during the spring of '84 for sufferers bet. Evansville & Wickliffe	Received from Steamer City of Frankfort.	Total number of rations received for the benefit of the flood sufferers, 1884.
		Rations.	Comforts.	Pairs of Blankets.							
1 Cavepoint, Ky			24	50							
2 Union Township, Ind											
3 Knight Township, Ind		5000	100	84	5000				5000		5000
4 West Franklin, Ind	1000	1000			2000				2000	500	2500
5 Alzey, Ky											
6 Pritchett's Landing, Ky										2500	2500
7 Crutchfield's											
8 Point Township, Ind											
9 Walnut Bend, Ky											
10 Mt Vernon, Ind	8500	8000			16500	10250	207	200	26750	5000	31750
11 Uniontown, Ky	15000	5700	151	100	20700				20700	3000	23700
12 Point Township, lower, Ind											
13 Raleigh, Ky	1000	1300	12		2300				2300		2300
14 Brown's Island, Ill											
15 Shawneetown, Ill	15000	12000	100	100	27000	40000			67000	2500	69500
16 Saline Landing, Ill							100		100		100
17 New Haven, Ill											
18 Mouth Saline River, Ill											
19 Blackburn, Ky		2000		50	2000				2000	250	2250
20 DeKoven, Ky		3000	25	50	3000				3000		3000
21 Coon's Ridge, Ky											
22 Cooper's Mines, Ky											
23 Davis' Mines, Ky											

www.ingramcontent.com/pod-product-compliance
Lightning Source LLC
Chambersburg PA
CBHW021523270326
41930CB00008B/1068